DEDICATION

This book is dedicated to two incredible people whom I love and miss every day of my life. BG and Missie, you will always be in my heart and not far from my thoughts.

ADVANCED PRAISE FOR *SHATTERED*

"What happens when your life is shattered...not once, but twice? My good friend Brenda Nevitt's honest and compelling story shows us that finding hope after devastating grief isn't easy, but it is possible. Her story inspires me to trust Christ no matter what events life throws at me because through her story I see how God strengthens us in the midst of the most challenging circumstances. Thank you for sharing your story, Brenda!"

- Kent Julian
www.liveitforward.com

"Brenda Nevitt has been a dear friend for over 20 years. Her husband, BG was the absolute best friend I could ask for. When he left us suddenly, Joyce and I asked ourselves: 'Now what will Brenda do?' We did not have to wait long, as she has pushed through the darkness, amazing everyone with her resiliency, passion to help others, by being brave and bold. She will inspire women across America in a thousand different ways, with her story of learning to live beyond the shattered dreams."

- Sam Johnson, Executive Director
Priority One Missions

"A great story written by an amazing new writer! Brenda writes as though she were telling their story to you. It reads as though you have no concept of where you are in place or time. The compelling side of the story makes the reader keep turning the page. The inspiration in it stays with you long after the book is finished."

- Drs. Dan and Jeanie Smith

ADVANCED PRAISE FOR *SHATTERED*

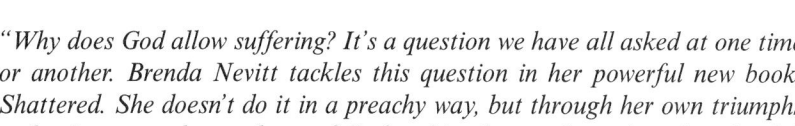

"Why does God allow suffering? It's a question we have all asked at one time or another. Brenda Nevitt tackles this question in her powerful new book, Shattered. She doesn't do it in a preachy way, but through her own triumphs and pain we see the goodness of God making beauty from the ashes that life can sometimes give us. This book encouraged me to keep trusting God...no matter what!"

- Pastor Matt Samuels, Lead Pastor
gtChurch

"Far more than a love story, Shattered is a life story. Your heart will be carried as you read the amazing victories that Brenda and her husband experienced in their life together. You will also weep as the tragedies of life begin to unfold. This is the true story of a woman who kept a grip on hope."

- Phil Schneider, Superintendent
Illinois District Assemblies of God

"'For I know the plans I have for you, declares the Lord.' These words have guided my friend, Brenda Nevitt, faithfully through her lifetime. Brenda is a living testimony to God's faithfulness and this book is written proof. It shares the journey of a man who lived life as one big adventure with God and the woman who, with God's help, managed to keep up with him. Through smiles and tears you will find yourself both encouraged and challenged. Encouraged by God's grace and the realization that you, too, can get through the tough times, and challenged to join in the journey and 'live like you are dying.'"

- Gerry Wakeland, President
CLASSEMINARS, Inc.

ABOUT THE AUTHOR

Brenda K. Nevitt is a survivor who has determined that her life will not be defined by tragedy.

Brenda is a speaker and pastor who has been in ministry for more than thirty years. She lives in Decatur, Illinois where she gets to spoil her two (soon to be three!) grandchildren. She is a natural encourager who loves to see people do well. When it comes to her favorite things, forget raindrops on roses and whiskers on kittens; Brenda loves peanut M&M's, Hallmark Christmas movies, and really good books.

Brenda is available to speak to church and community groups. Her messages bring hope and encouragement, especially to those who have experienced loss. Visit her website for more information.

BrendaNevitt.com

brendaknevitt@gmail.com

CONTENTS

Dedication 3
About the Author 6
Introduction 9
1. My Wish 11
2. First Comes Love 15
3. Then Comes Marriage .21
4. Then Comes the Baby Carriage 25
5. Change of Plans 29
6. Jumping Into Ministry .31
7. Never Say Never 35
8. They Said It Couldn't Be Done 41
9. Growing Pains 47
10. This is Going to Make a Great Story 61
11. An Adventure In the Sky 67
12. The Worst of Times 69
13. Roses and Leaves 75
14. My Big Red Chair 79
15. The Pistol-Packing Preacher 83
16. And It All Caved In 87
17. A Final Goodbye 93
18. This Was Not the Plan .99
19. One Step at a Time 105
20. Live Like You Were Dying 109

INTRO

*"And the **peace** of God, which transcends all **understanding**, will guard your hearts and your minds in Christ Jesus."* Philippians 4:7

Even now, it's hard to explain. In the midst of my life falling apart, I had a peace, a peace that only God can give. My day had started out just like any normal day. Now I was sitting in a small ER waiting room; one of those rooms reserved for family as they wait for news about a loved one.

The man I had been married to for thirty-six years had been in an accident and now I waited. I knew it was bad. As soon as I arrived at the hospital, they told me that BG was in critical condition, then showed me to this small waiting room with a small couch and a few chairs and a couple tissue boxes on a small table. The room would soon fill to overflowing with family and friends standing and sitting waiting for news.

I'm sure people around me wondered how I could remain so calm. It was a little hard for me to believe it. The future was uncertain. There were so many questions in my head.

What did critical condition mean?

Would the love of my life and best friend survive?

If he survived, would he be the same man I walked back up the stairs to tell, "I love ya, babe! See you later," just a few hours earlier?

But one prayer had changed everything. When I was notified about the accident, I immediately started shaking on the outside. I was trembling even more on the inside. That's when it happened. I found someone who would pray with me. As we prayed, the peace of God, which exceeds all understanding, washed over me.

As I sat in that waiting room, I just knew that no matter what news they would come to tell me, I would be all right.

MY WISH

Star light, Star bright

First star I see tonight

I wish I may, I wish I might

Have this wish I wish tonight.

I could see the stars right outside my window. Many times throughout my childhood, I had asthma attacks in the middle of the night. I would be awake and watching the stars outside my bedroom window. Because I couldn't breathe, it was impossible for me to lie down so I would sit up in bed, or sometimes my dad or mom would let me sit on their lap and rock just to try to calm my breathing so I could sleep. They would rub my back and tell me I was going to be all right. When I saw the stars out my window, I would sometimes wish that I wasn't sick anymore.

It's scary when you can't breathe, and sometimes those attacks were so severe that my mom and dad would have to get up and take me to the doctor who was thirty minutes away. He had an office in the lower level of his home and he could give me a shot. If the shot didn't work, we would drive another fifteen minutes to the hospital. It seemed like we were making that trip to the hospital over and over again. By the time I reached fourth grade, I literally spent more days in the hospital than I did in school. That's a lot of days!

I grew up in a great small town. Everyone pretty much knew everyone. Of course, that meant sometimes everyone also knew everyone else's business, but it was a good life in my small town. Dad managed the lumberyard and my mom stayed home with my sister and me. I'm sure she stayed home partly because of my physical challenges. I never heard my parents complain, but having a daughter who was continuously sick had to be very physically, emotionally, and financially draining.

One of the many things I admired about my parents is that they always helped me to think I could do anything in spite of all my health problems. I guess that's why when a friend asked me to go to church camp, my parents said yes. It was the summer right before I entered high school. The good news was that I wasn't as sick as I had been in fourth grade, but I still had many health problems. It is still surprising that my parents let me go because I was allergic to pretty much all of the outdoors.

Church camp was very new and exciting for me. I grew up going to church. Our family went to church because it was the right thing for my dad and his family to do as a businessman in the community. I had never seen people that were excited about God and enthusiastic about the opportunity to worship Him. I experienced this for the first time when I went to the camp church service.

One evening at the service, I decided I wanted more of God in my life. I went to the altar and prayed, and my life would never be the same. I went home a different girl than the one who went to camp. It wasn't that I had a huge transformation from "bad" girl to a "good" girl, but the difference that my parents noticed was the peace God gave me. When I had an asthma attack and I was struggling to breathe, instead of panicking, I felt an assurance that God would take care of me. In fact, after that night, many times I would picture God rocking me much like my parents had when I couldn't breathe. When things were falling apart, I could sense God just rubbing my back and whispering, "Brenda, you're going to be okay because no matter what happens I will be with you." And He has been! He's been there to hold my hand through some very difficult times.

A few months after attending camp, my friend Fern and I wanted to go to a church service. A group had come and put on a presentation at our school and was going to be at a church in a nearby town that evening. I begged my mom and dad to take us. My dad finally gave in. Fern and I were so excited!

On the way to the nearby town, my dad asked about what I thought the service would be like. Fern and I described the worship time, the message and the altar time. "Girls," my dad said, "Don't get any ideas about going up to the altar at the end of service. We will leave during that time. It's a school night and we need to get home."

But everything changes when God begins to work on someone's heart. Fern and I did not go up to the altar, but my dad did. He went forward and gave his heart to the Lord. We were the last ones to leave the church that night. My dad finally understood what God had done in my life. It was only a couple of months later when my mom and sister Gayle would also receive Christ. Wow! God had totally transformed my family!

You know, I'm sure the friend who invited me to church camp had no idea the impact that one invitation would have. After my immediate family members each made a decision to receive Christ, my grandma who was in her sixties also received Christ along with many of my aunts, uncles, and cousins. My dad and mom went into ministry. I got married and went into ministry. I think it would be safe to say that thousands of lives have been impacted by that one invitation. Wow! One invitation can make a huge difference!

Star light, Star bright

First star I see tonight

I wish I may, I wish I might

Have this wish I wish tonight.

At night, I was still gazing at the stars outside my window, but now I was thinking about a guy. I was wishing on a star that I would meet "the one." After I learned more about prayer, I would pray that I would meet that special guy. I just knew that God had that right guy for me. What I didn't realize was just how soon "the one" would come into my life.

FIRST COMES LOVE

I have a number of special dates I will always remember. My birthdate, my wedding date, the birth dates of my children.

Then there was July 28, 1974.

I had just turned sixteen and would be a junior in high school in the fall. A lot was changing in my life. My school was consolidating with another school, which meant I would go to school in a different town. My family was also changing churches. We had attended the same church all of my life, but my dad and mom were working with a group of people in the area to help a new church get started.

It was 1:30 in the afternoon on July 28. My family arrived at the church for the grand opening, which consisted of an open house in the afternoon followed by an evening service. We walked into the church and that's when I saw him. He wore a powder blue leisure suit and was standing at the front of the church singing with his mom and sister. Oh my goodness, he was cute and a singer!

After the open house, everyone who had worked on the church building shared a meal. My parents had worked many hours to help get the church finished. I sat across the room from the cute guy in the blue leisure suit. The room was crowded and there were a lot of people talking, so it was hard to hear what he was saying when he asked me a couple questions across the room. Then it happened. He walked across the room and sat down next to me. Ahh! He told me his name was BG Nevitt.

We soon discovered that not only would we be attending the same church, but also the same consolidated school! After the evening service, BG asked if I would like to get some ice cream. My mom and dad would not typically let me go out with someone I had just met, but they knew BG's parents and grandparents, so they let me go. We had to drive almost a half hour to a truck stop in a nearby town for ice cream. I was excited and nervous. I ordered a strawberry sundae and BG had a hot fudge. I started dating BG that summer and never dated anyone else.

I had no idea that would be a life-changing day. I thought I had met a great guy, but I didn't know he was "the one."

While I was a small town girl, BG was a city boy, at least until he was in junior high. That's when his family moved to a community about twenty minutes from my small town. He spent his early years in the Quad Cities. The Quad Cities are actually five cities right on the Iowa/Illinois border. Rock Island, Moline, and East Moline are on the Illinois side. Davenport and Bettendorf are in Iowa. Even when BG moved to the country and lived on a farm, there was something about him that always made him seem like a city boy. His dad was in construction and his mom was a beautician and owned her own shop. He had one younger sister, Glenda.

When school started in the fall, I quickly discovered some things about the guy I was dating. Everyone in school knew BG was a Christian and that he loved Jesus, and for the most part, they seemed to respect that. They would even call him Preacher sometimes.

BG had his own identity and was definitely not a conformist. He had his own fashion style, and didn't care that it wasn't what everyone was wearing. He was incredibly creative and his favorite class was creative writing. He was also very smart, though he didn't always make good grades—until he started dating me. Our parents wouldn't let us date on school nights, but we had a couple of classes together so we would often "need" to study together. We actually did study and BG made the honor roll for the very first time. After that, his parents decided our study dates were a great idea.

This smart, creative guy with his own sense of style also drove a unique car. If you took one look at our school parking lot, you could immediately spot BG's car—a 1956 Dodge Coronet Coupe. It was two-tone green with a push button transmission and steering wheel so huge I could hardly see over it. BG loved that car. Some years later the *Chicago Tribune* asked people to submit stories about their cars; BG's story was published. Here's the story he wrote:

"Ah, Dad!"

"There is no way that I am going to let you go see her again tonight. That is all you ever seem to think about anymore . . . Brenda, Brenda, Brenda. Well, not this time. You are going to get some things done around the farm. I have marked down the odometer reading, and I'll know if you go anywhere."

I knew my dad meant business, but you know how it is when you are young and in love. It was a forty-mile round trip to her house. How do you hide that? Disappointed and discouraged, I proceeded with my chores while out of the corner of my eye I watched my dad drive off to work. The first order of business: put the car away. Backing my dynamic 1956 Dodge coupe, equipped with a Red Ram V-8 and push-button automatic, down the lane to its parking place under the tree, the miraculous took place (or so it appeared to me). The odometer was actually going backward. This had to be an answer to prayer.

Like any love-struck sixteen-year-old who knew all the country back roads by heart, I backed that two-toned Dodge down twenty gravel miles and laughed with each vanishing mile. Though a challenging course, it was worth it. That car had provided a way for us to be together. As I drove home that evening, I was on top of the world – my dedicated '56 Dodge and I had beaten the system. Love (and Mopar) conquers all things.

It's true. BG actually drove that car backwards for twenty miles, and was only at my house for ten or fifteen minutes and we just stood out in my yard talking. I had found a guy who was very determined. He never told his dad about his little excursion until after we were married. When BG confessed, his dad looked at him and said, "Son, I'm so proud of you. I knew you would always find a way to do something if you put your mind to it. If I had found out back then, you would have been grounded, but now I'm just proud of you."

Through our junior and senior years of high school, neither of us had college in mind. BG wanted to get a job. He just knew he would be able to work himself up to a high level in some company. He had done that even in his summer job. BG started detasseling when he was in junior high. Detasseling is a job where you walk or ride on a machine through the rows taking the tassel off the ears of corn. As a kid, BG had always found ways to make money, but detasseling was his first official job and he was looking forward to his first day. He quickly found out that detasseling was very tiring and hot work. He came home from that first day in the field and told his dad he was going to quit.

"I knew you would never stick it out," his dad said. "I knew it would be too hard for you and you would quit."

Although that seems like a harsh thing to say, BG's dad knew him so very well. He knew that if he put it that way, it would challenge a young boy to decide to stick with it. BG decided right then to show his dad that he could do the job. And he did. Not only did he detassel every summer through junior high and high school, but he became a crew boss which meant more money. Even better, for two years he was the boss of his English teacher during detasseling season. Now that was fun.

BG was also an entrepreneur. He was always selling something. As a young boy he set up a carnival in his backyard and sold tickets to neighborhood children, and sold Santa Claus suckers at school. As a teen, he realized that those detasseling crews got hot and thirsty in the fields, so he decided to take a cooler with him each day and sell cold drinks.

As our high school days were quickly going by, we started to make plans for the future. BG was never crazy about studying, but he loved sales and business. I just wanted to get married to my high school sweetheart and live happily ever after. I began working as a bank teller the summer before my senior year, so I decided to stick with that.

After graduation, in the summer of 1976, BG took me out for the day to a beautiful area called Lake of the Woods. It has a picturesque lake surrounded by trees and trails. On one of those wooded trails, BG got down on one knee and asked me to marry him. Of course, I accepted immediately! To make sure we would always remember that special day, he carved our initials into the nearby tree. Oh what a romantic guy.

I was getting married! I was getting married to the guy of my dreams… my knight in shining armor… and we would live happily ever after. Everything would be perfect. Life would be wonderful all the time because we would be together!

Or so we thought as we looked toward our future!

THEN COMES MARRIAGE

I woke up that morning so very excited. It was our wedding day.

So much had happened the last few months and my head was spinning. At the end of our senior year, BG's parents had moved back to the Quad Cities and he moved with them. He got a job at a clothing store. I was still working at the bank and planned to move to the Quad Cities after the wedding. For months, we lived about three hours apart. On one visit, I decided to apply to a couple of banks in the Quad City area. At the first bank I went by to drop off my resume, they asked to do an interview and hired me on the spot. They wanted me to start right away so I moved in with BG's parents for a few months.

That's when my knight in shining armor found our castle—or maybe it was a mobile home. It was furnished and we could afford it. It was a start. Then just over a week before the wedding, BG lost his job. He went into work one day and they told him that the clothing store was closing. Some employees would be relocated to another store but since BG was the last hired, his job had been eliminated. But I was marrying one determined guy. He immediately started looking for a job. He really wanted to sell cars. He had one particular dealership in mind. He was determined to have a job before the wedding, so each day he made the rounds and filled out applications at all kinds of places. Then he would go to the car dealership where he really wanted to work, and each day they would tell him the same thing. "You are too young for this job. We are not going to hire you." Even though they told him no every day, he continued to stop by just to let them know how much he wanted the job.

On the Friday before our wedding, BG once again went to the car dealership and one more time the manager told him, "You're too young for the job. I'm not going to hire you." The owner of the dealership came in, noticed this young kid hanging around, and asked, "What's the story on that young guy?" The manager said, "He's driving me crazy. He wants to sell cars and so he comes and tells me every day what a great employee he would be." The owner turned to the manager and said, "Hire this guy. If he works half as hard at selling cars as he has trying to get this job, he will make us a lot of money." They hired BG and he worked the rest of that day until it was time for our wedding rehearsal.

As I woke up on Saturday, March 12, 1977, to get ready for my wedding, my future husband went to his new job. They let him take half a day off to get married. Our wedding was at two in the afternoon. BG worked all morning and even sold a car. As they were signing the paperwork, BG handed his customer the keys to her new car and an invitation to the wedding!

That man who sold his first car on his wedding day, serenaded his bride just a few hours later. We had searched and searched for the perfect song and I think we found it in *He has Chosen You for Me* by Pat Terry.

We don't know what tomorrow holds, but we know who holds tomorrow.

Knowing this we'll live above the world and all its sorrows.

I have prayed for all my life that we would be together.

Serving Him together seems so right.

Oh, oh yes, it's true.

He has chosen me for you.

Take my hand and we'll agree That He has chosen you for me.

As we said "I do", I had no idea how very true those words would prove to be.

The honeymoon for a couple with very little money and a brand new job consisted of going to a hotel in town for overnight before moving into our new mobile home (at least new to us). The next morning as we were seated for breakfast, we looked over and two tables away were my parents. Out of all the restaurants in the Quad Cities, who would have guessed that we would be at the same one as my parents?

We hadn't been married long when I discovered BG didn't always think the way I did. I'm sure I knew this when we were dating, but it seemed a lot different once we were married. One day when I came home from work, I heard a rustling in my kitchen. I stopped everything and listened. There it was again... the rustling. Then it happened. I saw a mouse run across the floor. I made a run for my bedroom, jumped on my bed, and immediately phoned my husband. I have an unexplainable—and I'm sure some would say totally unjustifiable—fear of mice. I was terrified but I just knew my knight in shining armor would rescue me.

"There's a mouse in the house and I need you to come home right now and do something about it!" I wailed through the phone. It was clear to me what would happen next. BG would go in and tell his boss that he needed to leave work immediately for a family emergency, because to his new wife this was an emergency! I needed help, not later, but now!

BG calmly told me there was nothing he could do. He couldn't go tell his boss that he needed to come home. He told me a little mouse was nothing to be afraid of. He also said he was really busy and needed to go, but he would be home in four or five hours, and would see what he could do then.

What? That's all he was going to say? Four or five hours? How was I going to survive? I needed that mouse out of my house that very minute! So I did what any sane person would do. I sat on my bed for four or five hours. Okay, I admit I did get off the bed for one bathroom emergency. I felt sorry for myself, and as you might have guessed already, there were plenty of tears.

When BG finally got home, I'm sure he was convinced he had a basket case on his hands. I could be reasonable about most things, but that was not the case with mice in my house. I don't remember how he finally caught the mouse, but I must admit that I feared mice the entire time we lived in our mobile home. In a rural area it was hard not to have mice and for me that was hard to live with.

BG had to learn to give me shots. I was still having asthma attacks and my parents had always given me shots when my asthma couldn't be controlled by oral medicine. I still remember telling BG that even though I had said yes to his proposal and accepted his ring, he was going to have to do one more thing before we could get married. At first, he wasn't sure if he could do it, but I had to have someone able to help me when I was very sick. Let me tell you, he was great about it. I would sometimes tease him and say, "You could be a nurse and give shots." He was so good that sometimes I would hardly feel the needle going in. What a blessing! I guess I got a man that was absolutely great with shots but not so great with mice!

THEN COMES THE BABY CARRIAGE

The first winter we were married was a particularly snowy one in the Quad Cities. For a very pregnant woman who didn't like to drive in bad weather, it was challenging. Yes, I said pregnant! About three or four months into our marriage we found out we were going to have a baby. We were thrilled. The hours we worked were great for a pregnant lady. I went into work early and most days would be home by about four in the afternoon. BG would typically not be home until nine or so, which meant I could go to work, come home and take a nap, and still be awake for at least a short time after he came home.

But why did it have to keep snowing? One day it snowed steadily while I was at work. That snow was on top of the snow that had fallen the night before. I drove home from work on slippery roads to discover they had cleared the streets in our development, but left a huge pile of snow that separated me from my home. By this time, I was very pregnant and very cautious on the snow and ice. I just sat looking at the huge pile of snow in front of our drive and tried to think of my options. I knew it would be hours before BG got home. All of our family was at work. Then I had an idea. I decided that if I kind of laid on the snow bank and just rolled over it, I could get to the other side and into my house. So that's what I did. I threw my purse and other bag over the pile and then I figured out a way to get myself on top of the snow pile and I rolled to the other side. If cell phones had been around, I'm sure you would have seen a video of the pregnant lady rolling over the snowbank on Facebook or YouTube.

Our baby was due the early part of March. We had just put a down payment on our first house. It looked like closing would be mid-February, which meant we would be in our new house and have fresh paint on the walls and the nursery done just before our new little one arrived.

Friday, February 3 was to be a late night for me at work. I was supposed to work until seven. I hadn't felt very good at all that day. My back hurt a lot. The girl who worked next to me had two children and said that most likely my body was just getting ready for the last few weeks before delivery. But in the afternoon, my supervisor told me to take off early. When I got to the house, I decided to call the doctor just to be sure I was okay. The doctor's office told me to come in and be checked. BG left work and picked me up. The doctor took one look at me, turned to BG and said, "Get to the hospital right now. I'll meet you there. She's going to have this baby today."

This wasn't supposed to happen for another month. We had absolutely nothing ready for a baby. I was planning to wait until after the move to stock the nursery. To top it off, my house was a mess because I hadn't felt well the day before either.

We got back in the car, and BG took off out of the doctor's parking lot, turned, and realized he couldn't think how to get to the hospital. He spotted a man walking his dog and yelled out the window, "Can you tell me how to get to the Silvis hospital? My wife is going to have a baby!" Fortunately, the gentleman knew the way and gave us directions.

At the hospital, they took me back to check me once again and get me ready to have this baby. BG went to call both of our parents, when the nurse ran to get him to let him know if he didn't hurry, he was going to miss the whole thing.

Though the doctors had given me medicine to try and slow her down, Amy Lynee Nevitt was determined and arrived at 5:44 p.m. After Amy was born, BG called my supervisor and one of my friends at the bank to let them know we had the baby. Of course, because he was always such a funny guy, they were sure he was just joking with them. Finally, after much convincing, they realized that it was true. I had left work a couple of hours before, and had gone and had a baby. We all decided it was a good thing they had let me off early, or I might have had the baby in the bank vault. That was the only place at the bank with a big table. Now that would have been a story!

You may have heard the saying that opposites attract. We could be the couple on the poster to illustrate that point. If you are familiar with the DiSC personality test, BG's the DI and I'm the SC. If you've read about the five love languages, again we are complete opposites. BG is the extrovert. I'm the introvert. BG is the leader. I'm the team player. BG loves to stand out. I love to blend in. So when it came to bringing our new baby home from the hospital, you should probably know that in a million years I would never have thought to do it in the way that BG did.

Just like any other new mom, the day I was discharged from the hospital, they put me in a wheelchair, handed me my brand new baby and wheeled me to the hospital entrance. I expected to come out of the hospital, get in our car, and make our way home. But I was married to BG, a guy who liked to do things in a big way. When the nurse pushed me outside, there was a group of people waiting for us including a camera crew from the local TV station. Everyone was there because BG had hired a chauffeur-driven limousine to take his wife and new baby home and the TV station was going to do a story about it. Back in those days, no one did anything that extreme. I must admit it was a bit overwhelming for me. We made stops at my bank as well as BG's car dealership. Then we made our way home. It had to be quite a site as we pulled up to our mobile home in our limo to begin our life with our precious Amy. This would have been another great video for social media.

Our youngest daughter, Melissa (Missie) Rae Nevitt, arrived just over two and half years later on September 18, 1980, and our family was complete. My doctor was very concerned that I wouldn't make it to the hospital to deliver the second baby so he put me on bed rest for two weeks before she was due. That was hard on everyone but especially Amy. When I arrived at the hospital to have baby number two, I told the nurses to pretend it was my first baby because I really didn't know what they normally did for a birth. With Amy, I'd changed into a hospital gown, got in bed and had a baby. Apparently, that is not normal.

Missie was completely different. She came in her own time. It's so interesting because in delivery, Amy came fast and she has always lived her life in a fast mode. Missie always loved to take her time and she was notorious for asking for two more minutes of sleep before she got up. I'm guessing she wanted the same thing when she was born.

As they wheeled me out of the hospital with my brand new baby, Missie, I was not surprised to see a limo waiting to take us home. After all, BG wouldn't do it for only one of his daughters. This time the TV crew was not waiting to film us. It was the newspaper photographer. They took a great picture of our two beautiful girls as we got into the limo to go home.

We were blessed with two wonderful little girls, one with curly hair and the other one with straight hair. One was the fashion girl and the other more the tomboy. They were two and a half years apart, but you would rarely see one without the other—complete opposites who would become best friends.

CHANGE OF PLANS

Life for our young family could be described in one word: busy. BG always worked a lot of hours, and I was working a full-time job and taking care of our little ones. BG had really become a workaholic. He was very driven and wanted to succeed in his career. I know that's why he did as well as he did at such a young age. He would later say how much he regretted working so many hours. He missed so much of the girls' young lives. Fortunately, BG's parents lived down the street and loved to help out with our family.

In the midst of our busy lives and trying to get ahead, BG started to lose his passion for God. It wasn't that he turned his back on God, it was more like he put that relationship on the back burner. He would miss church to go in and do extra work, or ask me if we could do something fun on a Sunday instead of attending church.

Shortly after Missie was born, a friend invited BG to his church. We discussed it and decided that it would be great for our family to try it. The first Sunday in that church, God was working on BG's heart. All of the sudden, it was just like old times except with a new freshness and zeal. BG was so excited about what God was doing. He started volunteering in all areas of the church. I decided to help with the nursery and toddlers because I had a baby and toddler. BG also began singing again, in church as well as at different events around the area.

Things were going well for BG in the business world. He was promoted to management at one of the largest car dealerships in the area. He was the youngest person ever to hold that position. It was quite an accomplishment. His bosses were very encouraging and kept telling BG they had plans for his future. But God had a different idea.

One Sunday night at church, BG remembered a time when he was ten years old and God was directing him into ministry. That night he was at the altar praying for a long time and we were among the last to leave church. We went home and put the girls to bed. BG told me he felt like he had really blown it with his life. He knew at an early age that he was destined for ministry and he had chosen business instead.

"Brenda, at the altar tonight, I told God I would do what He wants me to do. How do you feel about that?"

I told BG that I wanted to do what God wanted us to do with our lives.

"But I'm not sure what to do now," BG replied. "I know I can't quit my job, and go to Bible school with a wife and two children to support."

We decided we would do two things: we would say yes to God. And we would trust Him. We wanted whatever he wanted for our lives.

I had some concerns—fears, really—about ministry. My biggest fear was for my girls. I had seen some examples of pastors' kids who really suffered. I knew some kids who didn't even have a relationship with God and blamed it on their parents being in the ministry. I remember praying earnestly, "God, I'm willing to do anything you want me to do, but please keep my girls close to you. Please let them always love you and never resent the ministry."

We weren't sure what to do next, so we just tried to get ourselves ready for whatever God had for us. One morning, BG came into the kitchen and told me he felt that he was supposed to call his Grandpa Toliver and offer to help him in Jacksonville, Illinois. Grandpa T had come out of retirement for the second time to help a church whose pastor had died suddenly. It was a small congregation of mostly retirees. BG made the call and Grandpa T said, "I've been waiting for you to call me. I've been praying that you would come help me, but I didn't want to call and ask. I asked God to have you call me."

God had a plan. It wasn't the way we thought it would happen, but God was sending us to a church with almost no youth to be youth pastors. We had no idea what we are doing, but we were on our way to Jacksonville.

JUMPING INTO MINISTRY

Even though we were still trying to finish the packing, we weren't going to miss our last Sunday night service with our church. We arrived late because we were trying to load vehicles. A caravan would be moving us to Jacksonville, Illinois the next day. Sunday night service was always really packed, and we usually got there early so we could get a good seat. We finally found seats in the first row of the balcony overlooking the congregation seated downstairs. As we stood and sang, I reflected on our time there. BG and I had been attending this church for about four years and it had been a wonderful time in our lives. We had awesome pastors and we were going to miss their guidance, direction, and the fun times we'd had with them. We made some amazing friends at the church. Just after we started attending, we went to a newcomers' lunch and sat at a table with three other young couples who quickly became some of our best friends. We would miss them all so much. God had done some incredible things in our lives at this church. Now we were at our last service.

I looked out over the balcony and was suddenly filled with all sorts of emotions: sadness, excitement, nervousness, anticipation and a little fear. As the congregation sang, I had a talk with God. Not out loud but in my head. "God, I feel like I am stepping off this balcony. I know that you will be there to catch me. I know this is what we are supposed to do, but I also know that without your help this will never work. God, I love you and I trust you. I know you will not fail us."

It was a hilly and curvy drive from the Quad Cities to Jacksonville. Along the way, BG pulled into one of the small towns to mail our income taxes. It was April 15, 1982. As we mailed our taxes, I thought that the IRS might be surprised by the difference in our earnings the next year. We had given up good jobs to make this move. Jacksonville was going to be a big adjustment for us.

The church promised us sixty dollars a week.

Yes, sixty dollars a week in 1982 with two children! That was all the church to could afford to pay us but we knew that God would take care of us. BG was hoping to find a part-time job to help support our family. The larger car dealerships in town offered him jobs immediately but weren't willing to work with his schedule. That's when he decided to start working for a really small car lot near the church. He would be selling cars on straight commission but they were willing to work with the hours so he could actually do what he felt like God wanted him to do. Even though money was going to be very tight, we felt that I was supposed to stay home with our girls.

So our faith journey began. In the five years we had been married, there had been times that we really had to trust God for our finances but never like this. Each week in Jacksonville, we would pray that God would supply what we needed. And He did. Week after week, we had just enough. There was never any extra, but we made it.

During this time, we learned more about our finances than ever before. When we came to Jacksonville, we had some debt. We made enough money to make the payments, and that's what everybody did—right? If you wanted something and you had good credit, you just borrowed the money. We knew we needed to pay off that debt. I'm not sure how we did it, but in the four years we were in Jacksonville, we paid off all our debt and vowed never to go into debt again except for a house. If we couldn't pay for something, we would have to wait until we could afford to buy it. I will always be thankful for learning that lesson.

One week in particular was a really scary week for us financially. BG had not sold any cars and our sixty dollars went to pay a bill that was due. I had been praying all morning because I didn't have enough food to make a meal when we got home.

"God, you have been faithful before and I know you will somehow provide for us."

We drove home after visiting a family in our church and stopped at the mailbox. I was sure God would have someone send us some money to help us. But no check was in the mailbox. Then we pulled into the driveway and I saw it. On the porch were bags and bags of groceries. It was better than Christmas! We took those bags into the house and set them on the table and looked at all the wonderful things we'd be given. The crazy thing is that those bags were filled with things that our family loved! Things to make spaghetti, chicken and noodles and pizza were in the bags. We could even make brownies that night because our angel had given us all the ingredients, including the eggs. They had even included some candy for the girls! To this day, I have no idea what angel came and left those bags of groceries, but if you are reading this book, I want to say thank you from the bottom of my heart.

Jacksonville was a learning experience. Grandpa T was a great guy for BG to work for. He had been at the church for some time when we arrived. It was a good group, but they had very few younger people. Grandpa T has been in ministry long enough to know that you had to attract some younger people to the church or it would eventually die.

One incredible thing about Grandpa was he was always willing to let BG try almost anything. If BG had an idea, Grandpa would usually say, "Go for it." Not many older guys would have done that. I think Grandpa was determined that this would be a training time for him to invest in his grandson. And he did. BG always said that he learned more from Grandpa's school of ministry than anywhere he could have gone.

Since BG was the only staff person, he did all kinds of things. He led worship, directed the choir (which only worked because he had a great piano player who helped him), did some secretarial work, led the youth and young adults, started a prison ministry, started a church television program, and did a Sunday morning radio show. On top of all that, he sold cars.

During the time we lived in Jacksonville, my parents quit their jobs and moved to Tulsa, Oklahoma to go to Bible school to become pastors. Because our finances were so tight, I rarely saw them. One day, my grandma called and offered to pay for gas so we could make the drive to Tulsa. We loaded up the girls, and away we went. It was so great to see my parents but let me tell why that trip was so memorable.

In Tulsa, I had the opportunity to go to a church service. I don't remember much about the service except that at the end they offered to pray for people in need of healing. I was in my mid-twenties and still having quite a bit of trouble with asthma. Medical people had told me that sometimes you outgrow asthma but since I still had it, I would probably have it for the rest of my life. It wasn't as severe as when I was a kid, but even with medication, I still had some bad attacks that required BG to give me a shot. That night, I went to the front for prayer for healing. Many people had prayed for me for healing for my asthma in the past, but this time was different. I just KNEW that God had touched me that night and I was going to be totally healed. It wasn't an instantaneous healing but I just KNEW. I kept thanking God for my healing, and over the next few months, the asthma attacks became less frequent until they stopped. I was able to get off all my medicine. I WAS HEALED!

NEVER SAY NEVER

"All I know is that I never want to be a lead pastor."

A lot had happened in the time we had been in Jacksonville. The church added children's programs because young families were coming and attendance was growing. And we actually had youth! We typically had sixty to seventy kids at the youth group that had started with just a handful. It had been a wonderful, challenging, faith-building season, but we didn't feel we were supposed to stay.

BG talked to me about his options. He loved to tell people about Jesus. He was also a great singer. He thought that maybe God would open the door for him to travel as an evangelist. He had a list of other things in ministry that he would be open to doing but he definitely did not want to be the lead pastor at a church.

Only a matter of months after that conversation, Grandpa T told us he felt he wanted to retire again. Although we had loved our time in Jacksonville, we knew God was showing us that our time here was over. We would stay long enough to help the church find a new pastor, but what was next for our family?

It was not long before we were contacted by a church in Grayslake, Illinois. Grayslake is one of the far north Chicago suburbs. The church had been without a pastor for some time. They had heard about BG and were interested in talking to him about the possibility of being their next pastor. Although BG did not want to be a lead pastor, he desired more than anything to do what God wanted him to do. So we decided to visit Grayslake and talk to the people there.

When we arrived in Grayslake, we found a quaint smaller community. Although it most likely wouldn't be that way for long, because it was said to be the next Chicago suburb that would be seeing some real growth.

The Grayslake church had been in existence for seven years. They owned an old farmhouse and some land on the edge of town.

No church building. They were currently meeting in a school but it was a difficult situation and they really couldn't afford to pay the school. After we talked to them and BG looked at the financial situation, we weren't sure how they were going to pay us either.

But after a lot of prayer, BG and I both knew without a doubt, Grayslake was the place we were supposed to be. So in the fall of 1985, BG accepted the job as the lead pastor (or the only pastor on staff).

In the business world, you usually leave one company to go to another because you have an opportunity to take a step up in your career. That's not how it has been in ministry, at least for us. As we said yes to going to Grayslake, my practical mind said, "What are you thinking?" In Jacksonville, the church had finally grown enough so we were able to make a living without having to believe God for groceries on our doorstep. Now we were going to take another leap that was going to require a lot of faith.

One of my very favorite verses of Scripture is Jeremiah 29:11. *"For I know the plans I have for you," declares the Lord, "plans to prosper you and not to harm you, plans to give you hope and a future."* That verse had come to mean so very much to me as we had trusted God through our very first place of ministry in Jacksonville. I would need that verse even more in Grayslake.

BG quickly decided to stop meeting at the school and instead, to use what we had. We would take the old farmhouse and make it into a church. So we took out the walls and put beams on the ceiling to hold up the second floor. The downstairs was set up with church chairs, a sound system (under the microwave in the kitchen seating area), a very small platform, and a keyboard. All the usual things you would have in a church. Upstairs, there were two larger bedrooms, one really small room and a bathroom. One bedroom was separated into two classrooms, the small room became the nursery, and the other bedroom was where we lived.

Kind of crazy, right? We knew we needed to make some sacrifices until the finances turned around and the church could afford a building. A family in the church agreed to store most of our furniture and boxes. The rest of what we owned would be in that one bedroom. We had a bed, a TV, and a dresser. The girls, who were seven and five, would push a rollaway out of our room every night into the classroom. In the morning, they would get up and "make their bed" by folding it up and putting it back into our room.

Even though the setup was unusual, BG decided from the very beginning that we were going to function like a real church. We would have an order of service. We would have greeters and ushers. And we would start on time. This was something new. The church had been more laid back and would start whenever most of the people showed up. I still remember the day the keyboard player came in five minutes late and BG had started the service without her. He wasn't trying to be difficult, but he was trying to change the culture. If we wanted to attract more people and impact their faith, we needed to begin to function like a church even if we met in a house.

Living in the church was an adventure. Okay, let me tell you the truth: It was just plain hard, though we always called it an adventure. When we moved to Grayslake, we knew it was going to be difficult for our family for a time. I wanted my girls to love and serve God but also to love the ministry, so when we moved into the church we knew that how our girls handled our living situation was in our hands. It was our choice what their attitude would be, so we made a big decision—a really good decision. We decided that we weren't going to complain about living in the church.

Yes, on Tuesday mornings there was a group at my house at six in the morning for prayer. Yes, people stopped by at all hours because they didn't think of it as our home but as the church. And this meant that the church, which was my house, had to be clean at all times, even though we lived there with young children. Yes, Sunday mornings were nuts! I was running from the minute I got up. The girls had to be ready, the house picked up and the bathroom cleaned after the family was finished. And the most important thing, before people got there I had to be out of the bathroom! Because I was cleaning after everyone else got ready, I was the last one in the bathroom. I'll never forget the week someone came early. I was in the bathroom upstairs in my pajamas. To get to my bedroom, I needed to run across the stairway landing, which was visible from the front door. I waited at the top of the stairway and made the mad dash as soon as they moved away from the door.

There really were some legitimate things to complain about. The living conditions were difficult, with little privacy, and no money again. But we knew we could make it through because God had given us a vision of what He wanted to do in Grayslake and we were going to be part of that.

Our key phrase was, "Nobody else gets to do this." We told our girls, "You are the only ones who get to play church in the church." "You are the only ones that can help fold the bulletins every Saturday night." We used the phrase, "You're the only ones…" quite often. For Christmas when we had no money, our girls recorded a cassette using the church sound system. It makes it really convenient when the sound system sits right under my microwave. They made a cassette of all their favorite songs. It really was a great gift and they had a lot of fun creating that gift. It was definitely one of those things that no one else gets to do.

Through it all, God was growing our church. BG had managed to have the only display ad in the phone book directory under churches. You can imagine people's reactions when they arrived at Living Waters to discover it was in a house. We would see the cars stop at the end of the drive and pause. We were pretty sure the conversation in the car was something like this: "Could this be right? This church is in a house? Well, I guess since we are here, we could give it a try." What was really exciting was to see them come back the next week.

As we grew more excited about the church growing and people receiving Christ, something else incredible was happening in 1985. That would be Da Bears—the Chicago Bears. What a fun year to live in the Chicago suburbs! The Bears were winning a lot of games and the excitement was apparent everywhere you went. People proudly displayed banners and even refrigerator boxes outside of their homes. The refrigerator boxes were in honor of defensive lineman William "Refrigerator" Perry. Mike Ditka, the coach of the Bears, even lived in Grayslake! It was the year of the Super Bowl Shuffle as the Bears went all the way and won the Super Bowl!

Of course, we had an interesting way of watching the games. We didn't have cable so we had to use rabbit ears. Do you remember those? The TV in our bedroom didn't good reception. We had a TV on a cart that we used for church. We would sit in the plastic church chairs, eating our popcorn, and watching the Bears. What fun! That was my positive attitude coming out. A comfy chair or couch would have made the whole experience more enjoyable, but we were willing to put up with the plastic chairs because our Bears were winning!

As we continued to grow, we began to experience growing pains. A house can only accommodate so many people. We had two services in the house, but we were still experiencing some problems.

One problem happened on a Sunday morning. We had so many babies in our small nursery that people had taken all the furniture out of the room and set it in the hallway, and just sat on the floor and holding babies. We knew that we needed to do something. So BG came up with an idea. We would renovate the small garage behind the house. It was a real stretch to think that we could use the space. There was a hole in the roof and the building leaned to one side, but the guys all joined together and transformed that building into a nice room. We put heat and air in the building and officially named it The Ministry Center. This gave us an opportunity to move some of the older kids outside and move the nursery to a bigger room in the house.

One major problem was that the plumbing in the house was not made for so many people using the bathroom on a Sunday morning. So we did what anybody would do. We brought a port-a-potty and put it in our backyard for a few months. We then suggested that the guys use the outdoor facility and leave the indoor accommodations for the ladies. I know it sounds crazy but even with this crazy set up, people were still coming. Our record attendance for a Sunday in the house was 171. I'm not sure how we were able to squeeze that many people in that house, but God made a way.

To build a building on the property, we needed to raise $20,000. The first time BG talked about raising that much money, people immediately said it would never happen. The church had tried to raise $5,000 a few years earlier and had failed miserably. But they didn't know BG Nevitt. If BG was ever told, "There's no way," then he would become even more determined to find a way. And he did. He challenged people to give sacrificially. BG even began traveling and singing in churches. Any offering went to the building fund. People had yard sales, sold pizzas, and had car washes. As the building fund kept growing, people got more and more excited.

By summer, the building campaign was in full swing and doing well. We had decided to have a Vacation Bible School program for the kids. We invited everyone and oh my goodness, they came! VBS started on Monday and by Friday, we had more than 100 people in an old farmhouse! There were kids everywhere! After everyone went home on Friday afternoon, I was alone at the house (church) running the sweeper and picking up. All of those 100 kids would be coming back with their parents that night. The final program would be outside. We could never fit everyone in the house.

That's when it started to sprinkle. I just stood there looking out the window. There had been people at the church nonstop all week. I was exhausted and overwhelmed. And now rain. What were we going to do with all those people? It was too much!

That's when I called my mom and asked a very important question. "Mom, who do I call if the pastor's wife wants to resign?" She listened to my exhausted frustration. I'm not sure what she said, but I know she prayed with me. As I hung up the phone, I turned to look outside and the sun was shining brightly. I'm pretty sure God changed the forecast just for one very exhausted pastor's wife just to show her that He loved her and cared for her. That night, all the kids and parents came and we had a great program on the lawn. And I had survived it all!

THEY SAID IT COULDN'T BE DONE

We did it! They said it couldn't be done but we had raised more than $20,000. We were going to build a building. BG had done tons of research and planning, so when we finally hit our goal, he quickly put things in motion. He had met a contractor named Marty who traveled around the United States building Hardee's restaurants in thirty days. BG and Marty immediately clicked. BG was going to be very involved with the building of this church, and Marty was going to bring his crew in and make it all happen in thirty days.

I still remember the day the trucks started pulling in. The land had been prepared and the foundation poured weeks before, but we had no idea the trucks were coming that day. BG and I were leaving to go to a meeting when they pulled in hauling huge sections of walls. We pulled out lawn chairs and just sat together amazed as the sides of the church building we'd been dreaming of and praying for took shape before our eyes. We both had tears coming down our faces as we realized the goodness of God. It was really happening!

Would you believe it was actually done in thirty days? Marty had it down to a science. He had trade people come in for this part, and others come for another part. Many times the crews would work all night. Sometimes I would bake cookies and take them to the night crew. I always felt bad they had to work through the night even though BG told me it was just part of their job.

The church building was going up right next to the house and the girls quickly made friends with all of the workers. On a few occasions, they set up a lemonade stand. They always sold out of lemonade and cookies because the workers were so nice to them.

It was a beautiful building and it was finally done. A whole group of people was at the house to move everything over to our new church building so we would be ready for Sunday morning. As the last things were put into place and everyone was getting ready to go home, BG spoke up. "Hey guys, we have just one more thing to do. Can you stay around and help me? We want our furniture." In the excitement of the new church, most people had forgotten that we now had an empty house and could have our furniture back.

Until you have been without a comfy chair or a cozy couch for more than a year, you will never understand how we felt as our stuff came into the house. We were beyond excited. This would really be a new beginning for the church and for us. We would have our own home that we didn't have to share 24/7. I didn't realize how much I valued having some privacy. It had been a great faith-stretching experience but I was so thankful that we were going to have a church and a home and they would be in different buildings.

A week after we moved into our new building, a woman who volunteered in the office talked to BG and me about our health. Neither one of us had been feeling good for a few weeks, but we were too busy to be sick so we just kept going. Tina told us both that we needed to see a doctor. That's when I realized once again how good God had been to us through our first year in Grayslake. When Tina asked me who my doctor was, I told her we didn't have a doctor. We hadn't needed a doctor because for well over a year, no one in our family had been sick. That was totally God's provision. We had no money and God had supplied health.

Now we were coughing, congested, and sick. Tina called her own doctor's office and they made room to see us that very afternoon. Before we knew it, we were in exam rooms right next to each other. I was scared. I could hear BG coughing and I didn't sound much better. What was this going to cost? I heard them say something about taking an x-ray because BG's cough was so bad.

"Oh, my goodness, I wonder if they take payment plans?" was going through my mind.

Tina had made this happen so quickly. I wasn't sure if I'd told her that we had no insurance. The church was doing better, but there still wasn't enough money for us to have any kind of insurance. I knew I hadn't told her that we didn't have the money to pay for a doctor. I was praying for healing and for financial provision when the doctor came into to see me. I had a bad sinus infection. BG had pneumonia.

The doctor was nice and even gave us some samples of medicine to take. Then we headed out to the reception desk. I was dreading the news. I knew this would be expensive, especially with the x-ray.

I went to the window and the woman looked up from her typing and said, "Thanks so much. Hope you feel better." I paused and looked at her, "What do I owe you for today?"

"There's no charge for today."

I just stood there. "Did you say there's no charge for today?"

She said, "Yes."

We went to the car and sat there in amazement. Then I started crying because once again, God had provided in a way that we could hardly believe. He had answered my prayer and poured an incredible, unexpected blessing into our lives.

It was a great time in our lives. We loved living in Grayslake. Our new church building was awesome, and God was blessing the ministry. We added a second service as people continued to come. They were starting plans to build 3,500 homes right in the area around our church. We knew the families who moved to the area would be looking for a church. Our girls loved their school. BG and I had always believed that it was important to put down roots in your community and stay in the community to build a great church. We were going to be in Grayslake for the rest of our lives. That was our plan.

But that wasn't God's plan. In late spring 1991, I told BG about a dream I kept having. "I think God is telling me that I need to clean my closets because we're going to be moving." He looked at me like husbands sometimes do and said, "Brenda, we are not moving." I said, "Ok, but I think I'll start cleaning my closets just in case."

It was sometime in July when two couples from Decatur, Illinois visited our church. It wasn't unusual for us to have people from out of town visit the church. After all, we were just minutes from Great America, which is a very popular theme park. I didn't meet the two couples, but BG talked to them for a while after the service.

A week later on Saturday night BG had just gotten home from putting the last touches on his message when the phone rang. It was a deacon from the church in Decatur. He was one of the men that had visited the church the week before.

"Pastor BG, we were wondering if you would consider coming to be the pastor at Glad Tidings in Decatur?" Without hesitating, BG said, "No thank you."

When he got off the phone I reminded BG about the closets. "Honey, remember the dream that I keep having? Maybe you better pray about it." He didn't want to pray about it, and neither did I. We loved where we were. It hadn't always been smooth sailing but that's true anywhere you go. We both are fiercely loyal so it was difficult to think about ever leaving.

God continued to work on our hearts, especially BG's. He finally called and talked to the deacon in Decatur and set up a meeting. In his words, "I wanted to see what I was praying about."

We left the girls with friends and headed for the meeting in Decatur. As we entered the city on Route 51, BG said, "Oh dear God, please don't make me come here." It really had nothing to do with the city, the people, or the church. We just didn't want to move.

The meeting with the deacons went well—really too well. It had us in such a tizzy that we couldn't sleep. We were staying in a hotel that night, but since we couldn't sleep, we got up and drove home. As the miles passed, we continued to talk and the more we talked and prayed, we knew God was leading us to Decatur.

"Maybe God just wants to see if we will be obedient no matter what is asked."

"Maybe we will go interview and they will vote no and we can just go home."

We were in the car with our girls heading to Decatur to interview at a church where we did not want to go. People were very kind to us all weekend. BG preached in the morning. In the evening, everyone came back for a question and answer time. BG told me that he wasn't going to sugar coat anything. He would tell them if he came to Decatur, there would have to be some major changes. After he laid everything out, we went back to the office so they could vote. We were honestly praying the church would vote no.

The vote was unanimous. BG was the new pastor at Glad Tidings in Decatur. Our family was truly devastated because it was going to be so hard to leave Grayslake. How were we going to tell our wonderful congregation that we were leaving? So many of them had received Jesus as their Savior right there in the church. How would they respond to this news?

I was glad I had my closets cleaned out. I knew it was going to be hard to leave, but when God showed us we should go, we needed to obey.

Decatur, Illinois, here we come!

GROWING PAINS

"It was the best of times. It was the worst of times."

This quote from Charles Dickens' *A Tale of Two Cities* perfectly describes our time in Decatur.

I was very concerned about this transition for our girls. Amy was entering eighth grade and Missie fifth grade that fall. They didn't want to leave their friends or their church in Grayslake. But on the Monday morning after the vote, God did something very special for our girls. Our little dog had been run over several weeks before and our family had been devastated by the loss. We had been looking for another Yorkie for some time. That morning before we left Decatur to go back to Grayslake, BG looked in the paper and saw an ad for a two-year-old Yorkie. The dog sounded perfect so BG called right away. The dog hadn't been sold which seemed amazing because the ad was in the Sunday paper and it was already Monday morning. We went to see the dog and immediately fell in love with little Olivia. And we could afford to pay for her! We were just handing our money to the owner when someone came running up to the door wanting the dog sight unseen. But God had kept that little dog for my girls. He knew that that little dog would be just what the girls needed for this traumatic move. I love how God sometimes thinks of the little things in life that can be a blessing. I was so grateful for that dog. Throughout the years, we have had several Yorkies, but by far, our little Olivia was the smartest and the best behaved and just what our girls needed at the time.

Our first official Sunday at Glad Tidings Church was September 8, 1991. Glad Tidings was a lot smaller than the church in Grayslake and had been in decline for a while. We had a wonderful group of people to work with and BG began to make changes immediately. One of our first priorities was to improve the look of the church. The worship center desperately needed help. The pews were in really bad shape and the lighting was terrible. As we raised money and made improvements, God began to do something in the hearts of the people. BG had an incredible vision for reaching people who didn't know Jesus and he worked to instill that in our people.

Our slogan was, "It's worth the drive for a church that's alive. Conveniently located across from the Decatur airport." When we started printing that slogan, I'm not sure that our church was really alive yet but we were on our way. I always loved that we were "conveniently located across from the Decatur airport." It was very convenient if you were flying to church. But the people in our congregation began to get excited and new people began to come.

They call it "the honeymoon." When a new pastor arrives at a church, there is usually a happy season when things go very smoothly. Sometimes the honeymoon even lasts through the first year, but ours ended abruptly. We had just hired a youth pastor and finally felt that we could take a few days away to go see BG's family. While we were away, gossip about BG and our family began to spread through our congregation. It was so bad that our youth pastor, Brian, called BG in North Carolina. We cut our vacation short and drove home. BG was composing his letter of resignation in his head during the twelve-hour drive. As soon as we got back to Decatur, he went to the church and wrote his resignation letter. Then, after a few hours in prayer, BG tore up the letter. He had never quit anything because it was too hard and wasn't about to start now.

There are times when we just have to hold on to what we know God wants us to do. Somehow, we get it in our minds that if God has called us to do something, it will be easy. It will go smoothly. I'm not sure where any of us get that concept, but nothing could be further from the truth. I'm more and more convinced that too many times people give up way too soon on the dream that God has put into their hearts, just because it starts to get hard. Often what we really need to do is just hold on through the tough times, because God has great things ahead.

So we did. We held on to the dream and the vision for what God wanted to do in Decatur, and God began to turn things around. It still wasn't easy but God was doing some incredible things in the lives of people. The church was growing and had been able to add a music pastor along with the youth pastor. Now one of our problems was trying to find room for all of the people that God was bringing. What a great problem to have. Soon we added a second service, and later a third.

Many changes had taken place at the church. Now it was time for one more big change. It was time to change the name of the church. We were a contemporary church with an old-fashioned name. The name, Glad Tidings, was popular in the 1950s, but we had to find some way to give it a new contemporary feel. As we considered new names, someone suggested GT Church. It was simple. It was contemporary. It was perfect!

When we moved to Decatur, BG made one major change in his lifestyle. He was finally taking a day off! That was a huge thing. I was married to a workaholic who was driven by the dream God had put in his heart, and he didn't know how to slow down. He had never had an official day off. He would take time to spend with the family but never a designated day. Before we made the move to Decatur, I told BG, "Let's start from the very beginning to have a designated day off. If you have to work occasionally on that day, no problem. But let's set it up from the very start." So Mondays were the designated day and Monday nights were always family night. No one made any other plans because we were going to spend that time together. At first, it was hard for BG not to be at the church on Monday mornings, but he later told me it was one of the best decisions he ever made. Well, maybe the best decision his wife pushed him to make. It probably saved him from burn-out.

It was time for us to start looking for a house of our own. We had lived in church parsonages in Grayslake and Decatur for more than ten years. We began looking for a home in November. It's not a busy time for real estate that close to the holidays and we thought someone might give us a good deal during the winter months. We were the perfect buyers. We had a down payment, an approved loan, and no house to sell.

We found a home that we loved but it was way over our budget. The beautiful English Tudor, set back from the street and surrounded by trees, was just minutes from our church. It was empty and had been on the market for a while. BG kept telling me we were going to get that house. I must confess I had my doubts. I loved the house but they wanted so much more than we could afford. BG finally said, "Let's make them an offer. All they can say is no." So we made an offer and they said no. As a matter of fact, it was so low that they were offended.

But BG was sure that house was supposed to be ours and he was determined to get it. It took two months of negotiating but they finally agreed to sell us that beautiful house. As we signed the papers, the seller and his wife sat across from us, and he was angry. He kept saying, "I can't believe I'm selling you this house for this low price." I could believe it. God was providing for us.

I must tell you about a promise that God made to me years before. We had moved to Grayslake and had just sold our house in Jacksonville. BG and I felt we were supposed to give the money we had received from the sale of our house to help the church in Grayslake. We were obedient and gave our money. Shortly after we gave the money, we attended a large church service in a nearby town. At the end of the service, I went forward for prayer. I asked for prayer for family and the church. I did not know the person who prayed for me that night, but before I went back to my seat, she said, "I believe God is saying to you, 'I see your obedience and your sacrifices and I will bless you for those sacrifices.'" I hadn't thought about that prayer for years, but as we put the key in the door of our new home, God brought that promise of blessing to my mind. He had provided a home that was more than we could ever imagine.

God was blessing GT so much that it soon apparent we were going to need a bigger worship center. We had a very cramped worship area with an incredibly small foyer. It was so crowded in the foyer that we could hardly let people out of one service so others could come in. We decided to turn the gymnasium located in the back of the property into a worship center. Everyone was so excited as we broke ground for expansion. BG was one of the few pastors I know who loved to build buildings. His dad was a carpenter so he had always been around construction. He loved to be a part of everything and worked hard to be sure things were done just right. BG designed the building to have a huge atrium with room for people to talk and gather. The whole building was a complete answer to prayer.

GT was growing, and our girls were growing up. And I wasn't ready for it. Amy was a senior and Missie was a freshman in high school when it hit me. I was driving home after a funeral, when I suddenly felt overwhelmed with all kinds of emotions. My baby girls were growing up and would be out of the house soon. What would I do? I did a lot at the church, but my main title had always been Mom. God had been so faithful to me. Amy and Missie loved Jesus and loved being a part of ministry at the church, which had been my prayer from the beginning. But it wouldn't be long until they would be leaving our home for lives of their own and I wasn't ready. I cried as I was drove across town, pouring out my heart to God and asking Him to help me be ready for what was next. And that's exactly what He did. Right there in that car, He brought me peace and assured me that when the time came, I would be ready. It might be hard but I would always be Mom no matter what. He also assured me that when the time came, He would have more for me to do.

From the beginning, my role at GT was behind the scenes. I was willing to work with kids and do anything that needed to be done as long as I didn't have to be in front of people. I hated being in front of a group of people. I would get so nervous that I could hardly remember what I needed to say. What I didn't know was that as my girls were growing up, God was preparing me to stretch my faith and come out from behind the scenes.

After high school, Amy decided she would like to be a teacher. But at the end of her second year in college, she came home and told us that God had spoken to her heart. She was supposed to go into ministry. What a huge surprise! Although Amy loved to volunteer at the church, she had said, "I don't want to be in ministry or marry a pastor. I just want to be a volunteer." Oh Amy, you should never say never.

Amy took a year off to teach at a preschool, but soon joined the staff at GT as one of the Children's Directors. Missie was unsure what she wanted to do after high school. She worked a couple jobs but finally realized her passion was making people beautiful on the outside. So she enrolled in cosmetology school. Her second "job" was volunteering in GT's children's department. Both of the girls loved kids which made them popular at church and in high demand as babysitters.

Amy and Missie had always been best friends ever since they were little. I would even have people comment that they had never seen sisters so close. That bond continued as they grew up. I guess you could say they were Best Friends Forever. They did everything together. So it was no surprise when they decided to share an apartment. They had so much fun decorating it and loved to have friends over to their own place.

God had blessed me with two wonderful girls who were growing up to be incredible women who loved God. Those prayers that they would grow up to love God and the ministry were answered in an incredible way!

With my sister Gayle.
I am the older sister.

With BG at our junior prom.
My date was the cutest guy
in the school.

March 12, 1977 – We're getting married!

And baby Amy makes three.

1980 – The newspaper took our picture as we left the hospital and got into our chauffeur driven limo.

Two awesome girls – one with curly hair and one with straight.

Matching shirts for everyone. The back of the shirt said "BG's Bunch".

Easter Sunday always meant pretty dresses, hats, and white gloves.

1985 – Our last year in Jacksonville, Illinois. The girls were growing so fast. Amy was in second grade and Missie was in her last year of preschool.

Our first year in Decatur. Amy was in eighth grade and Missie in fifth. I prayed they would grow to love Decatur as much as they loved Grayslake.

Lots of fun memories with the 1964 Mustang. We had to take one more picture before we sold it. The money went to our church building program.

Missy & Amy—Best friends forever.

Our last family picture before Missie died.

BG always believed in having fun. We had just had our picture taken for something at the church. Then BG decided we needed to have a fun picture. Now it's one of my favorites.

Our girl getting married! We were so happy, yet it was sad without a special sister to share it with.

Ella Rae Grove —How can one little girl bring so much joy?

Sixteen months later, and there were two bundles of joy—Ella and Bennet.

What a fun Christmas! Two grandchildren equals lots of fun. We had no idea this would be our last family picture with BG.

My big red chair is the perfect place to read stories to Ella and Bennett. God gave me the desires of my heart.

In spite of the missing two special people in my life, I am blessed with a wonderful family.

THIS IS GOING TO MAKE A GREAT STORY

As we settled into our life and ministry in Decatur, BG had the opportunity to travel. Whether he traveled across the United States to attend a meeting or he flew across the world for a mission trip, he loved the adventure of traveling, and the stories that those travels might hold.

Nobody loved a great story more than BG Nevitt. He loved to tell stories, and people loved to hear him tell his stories. Whether during a Sunday morning message or just sitting at a dinner table, he could make the simplest story captivating.

"This is going to make a great story," is a phrase that BG often used. Instead of being discouraged and beaten down by circumstances, BG believed that God could and would turn things around and would make a great story. Crazy things seemed to happen to BG and every time they happened, he felt that God must really love him because this was going to give him another story to tell. In the next few pages, I am going to share a couple of his all-time favorites.

One day my phone rang while I was cleaning our bonus room. This was the room above the garage which seemed to be the catchall. If we didn't know what to do with something, we put it in the bonus room. BG was on a mission trip, which meant this was a perfect time for me to get rid of some stuff. BG didn't like to get rid of anything. He always said, "I might need that sometime." I was just starting to make my save, sell, or throw away piles, when my phone rang. My caller id showed it was an international call. It was very unusual for BG to call me when he traveled internationally. This was before cell phones so it was usually very expensive to make calls.

I was a little apprehensive when I answered the phone, concerned that there might be a problem in Georgia. BG was not in the state of Georgia. He was in the Republic of Georgia. Georgia is a tiny country in the middle of Russia, Armenia, and Turkey. It was part of the former Soviet Republic. BG was in the country with a group of pastors to speak at a leadership conference.

"Hi honey, I just wanted to let you know that everything is going good in Georgia. The leadership conference went really well. We had a small problem with a group of people who weren't happy about Christian pastors from America being in the country. The press even did a story about it. We are all fine. I just wanted to let you know in case any news agency would show the story. I'll tell you all about it when I'm home in a couple days. Love you!"

Apparently, that's the story you should tell your wife when you are in another country and you don't want her to worry.

Here's what really happened.

The leadership conference had been going really well with a few hundred people in attendance. On Friday, members of a group from Georgia's Orthodox Church tried to push their way into the conference to disrupt it. This rebellious group, led by defrocked priest Basili Mkalavishvili, was known for attacking religious groups. They felt any group that was not the true and real Orthodox faith was satanic. They had broken into services and meetings in the past and had even drug people out into the streets. There had been times they had beaten the Christians and burned all their Bibles and literature.

The local Christians, knowing that this was a constant threat, kept the doors barred when they met and positioned people at doorways and windows to watch for anyone who might try to break in. They knew exactly what to do. If there was any trouble, they immediately scooped up the children and put them into hiding. They also gathered the Bibles and hid them for safekeeping.

That Friday during the conference, there was a lot of shouting and intimidation outside and a mob of people tried to force their way into the meeting. When they couldn't enter, they damaged some vehicles parked outside. They posted notices on the vehicles and on the doors of the building giving strict warning never to meet again. Although the group threatened to come back later in the day with a larger mob, they did not.

The pastors who were in Georgia were all a part of an organization called Priority One. Priority One is a group that works to help build Bible schools all over the world. On Saturday morning, the pastors set out to see a piece of property where they hoped to build a Bible School in Georgia.

They had begun to walk around the property to see where buildings would be located, when a car suddenly pulled up behind them, honked its horn, and Mkalavishvili and some of his strongmen got out. They rang a bell and out of nowhere, more than 100 people converged yelling and screaming! They immediately starting hitting and beating the pastors! BG is over six-foot-two—not a little guy—but before he knew it he was pushed to the ground as people swarmed him and the other pastors. His cameras were taken, and his glasses were broken as he was repeatedly hit and kicked. The mob beat the pastors with rocks, sticks, clubs, and fists. BG kept trying to turn his head to keep from being kicked in the face, but no matter which way he turned, another boot was there. Every time he tried to get up, they would push him to the ground and continue the beating.

At some point the beating stopped. They yanked BG up, wiped his face with a dirty rag, then put a video camera in his face and started saying something he could not understand. He would later find out the rebels said a group of pastors had attacked them.

A small white car then came down the street driven by a man who had attended the leadership conference and recognized the pastors. He immediately started yelling at the rebels. This caused the attackers to disperse. They had made their point.

Three or four of the pastors immediately got into the little white car and quickly made their way back to the hotel. The rest of the group walked down the street to get on the bus that had brought them to the area, but it wasn't there. When the trouble broke out, the bus driver had taken off. The pastors had to walk for a while to find the bus and convince the driver to take them back to the hotel.

When they arrived back at the hotel, they assessed the damage. Several pastors were injured, but BG seemed to be one of worst. His finger appeared to be broken. This radical "religious" group had been persecuting the church in Georgia for a very long time, but this was the first time that any foreigners had been involved in the attack. Some men from the American embassy and the Georgia press came to talk to the pastors. The headline "American Pastors Beaten Up" appeared in the paper the next day.

BG was taken to the hospital in Georgia to have his hand looked at. He was shown into a room to be x-rayed. Everyone waiting for an x-ray sat in a room watching others being x-rayed. The x-ray table was a sheet of plywood. The room had a single light bulb on a cord. There was a soldier with a broken leg in the room. To get the soldier on the x-ray table, other patients had to assist him. BG was finally x-rayed, then called into the next room to talk to the doctors. The doctors sat across a table from BG, smoke from their cigarettes hitting him in the face. The break was bad and BG needed surgery for the bone to heal correctly. They wanted to set up a time to do the surgery. BG politely told them, "Thank you so much for your help, but I think I will wait to see my doctor and have the surgery when I get back home."

After he left the hospital, BG was taken to the police department. He was the only one in the group with documentation to show he had been physically hurt in the attack. People from the church wanted him to go give a statement to the authorities. The church in Georgia thought that documentation of an American being attacked would go a long way toward helping them fight for the religious freedom they were supposed to have.

Within a few days, the pastors were on a plane headed home to the United States. Sam, the leader of Priority One, apologized for taking them to an area where they would be in such danger. BG always told me he considered it an honor. "Not many of us ever experience the persecution that many people in this world face on a regular basis. If what we experienced helped the persecuted church in any way, it was worth it."

And it did. God used the persecution those men experienced and turned it for good. It was not long after their experience that a new leader was put into power. We happened to hear about it on the radio on a Sunday morning on our way home from church. There had been a peaceful take over of the government in Georgia. Mikhail

Saakashvili, who had received his college education in the United States and was a leader in the country of Georgia, had been placed in power. He would soon hear of what the Americans experienced and further hear of the persecution that the church in Georgia was experiencing and he did something about it. He declared that there would be religious freedom in Georgia. Members of the group that attacked the pastors were arrested and put in jail. And a beautiful Bible school has been built on the property where the attack took place. God is so good!

BG had a great story to tell. He was in terrible pain as he traveled back home, but he knew that God was going to use this story. He told the story to the press, his church, and many others. He came home, had surgery on his hand, got new glasses so he could see again, and totally healed up, but he would always say, "God blessed me with an incredible experience and a great story."

AN ADVENTURE IN THE SKY

BG didn't have to be in a different country for crazy and interesting things to happen to him. I must admit, I'm glad there were times I didn't know everything that he experienced until after it was all done and God had "rescued" him. At least in this adventure, he didn't have as far to travel home.

It was about eight in the evening. when I came home and saw the light on the answering machine was blinking. I hit the message button and immediately heard BG's voice.

"Hi Bren, I just wanted to let you know that we've had a slight change in plans. We decided to drive home instead of fly. We aren't getting a very early start back but I should be home in a few hours."

After I listened to the message, I turned to my girls and said, "There's a whole lot more to that story than what he's saying. They wouldn't just decide to drive when they flew this morning." And I was right. There was a lot more to the story.

The morning was beautiful. It was the perfect day to fly. BG and Kraig, one of our staff pastors, had an appointment to meet with a pastor in Muncie, Indiana. They had originally planned to drive, but BG had a friend who owned a small plane and was always looking for an opportunity to take it up in the air.

BG loved to fly. He really wanted to get his pilot's license and his friend had even begun to give BG some flying lessons. At the airport, Kraig took one of the back seats in the plane and BG went immediately to the copilot seat. The flight to Muncie was picture perfect. They landed in Muncie and headed to their meeting with the pastor. The meeting went great. Now all that was left was a nice fight home.

Take off was smooth. But not long after they were in the air, the engine started to make some weird noises. The pilot told BG to pull out the map and look for a place for him to set the plane down. BG was quickly searching the map and praying when he looked out the windshield and saw a spark and a puff of smoke. Suddenly the propeller stopped. BG immediately thought to himself, "I don't know a lot about planes, but I'm pretty sure the propeller should be turning."

At some point, BG threw the map over the back of his seat. He didn't need a map now. He could search with his eyes because they were getting close to the ground. The plane was dropping at a fast rate of speed. The pilot was trying to maintain control, when it appeared—a small landing strip in the middle of nowhere. That plane stretched out its landing gear and just barely made it onto that landing strip. That plane had landed safely! It was a true miracle!

The farmer who owned the small landing strip had seen the plane and came out to see if everyone was ok. As they talked about the harrowing experience, they asked the farmer why he had a landing strip on his farm.

"I built that landing strip back in 1958. Haven't used it much lately."

"Well, I'm pretty sure that I know exactly why you built that landing strip," BG immediately said. "I was born in 1958 and God knew that in 2003, I was going to be in a plane that needed to make an emergency landing. Thanks so much for building that landing strip."

Over the years, I have learned that my husband loved an adventure and I think God loved to give him adventures. There are times in our lives when we play it too safe. At least I do. We are afraid to do something new or to venture into the unknown. We want everything to be the same with no changes in our plans, but I think I have learned from BG that our plans may change. Things might not be how we want them to be, but if we continue to trust God, He's going to give us some great stories.

THE WORST OF TIMES

Sometimes the stories we have to tell are not the ones we want, ones we would never choose.

It was one of those weeks—so busy I could hardly keep up with everything. The church had recently purchased an old Kmart building as a second location. It was not far from our current facility but it would give us an opportunity to add additional services and accommodate more people. We were planning a banquet in that old K-Mart to raise money for the renovation. A banquet in a building that had been vacant for more than two years was quite an undertaking. Teams of people had been working for weeks to get the facility cleaned so we could use it. My daughter, Amy, and I were working with a team on the many details that still had to happen before this dinner could take place.

We were a week away from the big day, when my phone rang. It was Missie. She was so excited. She had just received a belated birthday card with some money from her aunt and uncle. Missie had turned twenty-four a few weeks earlier. She was going to cosmetology school and working part time at Cracker Barrel. She rarely had money just for fun shopping, so you can imagine her excitement when this "fashion girl" could go look for some new clothes.

"Mom, let's make it a girl's day. How about you, Amy, and I go shopping and then out to lunch?"

I hesitated. I knew I had to give a presentation to volunteers on Sunday morning and I wasn't ready. Getting up in front of adults was always so hard for me. I really needed to be sure I was comfortable with my presentation. But before I said no, a thought went through my head. How many twenty-four-year-old girls want their mom to come along for a shopping trip? So I told Missie I would love to shop with her in the morning and then have lunch, but I would need to come home after that to get some work done.

Saturday morning we headed to the mall and had an absolutely fabulous time. Missie was a bargain hunter and made her birthday money stretch. After lunch, I dropped the girls off by their car and headed across town. As I sat at the stoplight, I thought, "What a great day! God, thank you for giving me such wonderful girls. Thank you that we like to spend time together. I'm so glad that I made time to do this today."

I had no idea how very special that day really was.

The next day was a beautiful Sunday morning. I saw Missie for my usual Sunday morning hug. She told me that she would be going into work later that day. About 9:30 that night she called and said she really didn't feel well and she wasn't sure she would be able to go to school the next day. Missie loved cosmetology school and couldn't wait to graduate and be able to do hair every day. She hated that she might miss a day of school.

Monday and Tuesday were a blur of activity with banquet details. We were working until eight or nine every night. I knew Missie had not been able to go to school on Monday or Tuesday. I tried to call her a couple of times but she hadn't answered. I wasn't surprised. When Missie didn't feel well, she always slept a lot. I sent soup and 7up home with Amy to be sure Missie kept hydrated.

On Wednesday morning as BG and I were getting ready to go to the church, Amy called.

"Mom, I don't know what's wrong with Missie. She's looking at me, but she's not talking at all. I think you and Dad should come over."

BG and I jumped in the car and headed across town. As soon as we entered the apartment, we immediately knew something was very wrong. Kraig, one of our staff pastors and the girls' friend and neighbor, helped us get Missie to the car and we rushed to the emergency room. There have been times when I have arrived at an emergency room, and people didn't move as if it's an emergency. In fact, there have been times when I have had to wait quite a while to be treated in an emergency room. But as soon as they saw us trying to bring Missie in, they immediately ran to help and began to work on her.

Sometime later, the ER staff came to the waiting room.

"It's possible that it is meningitis. We are moving Missie to ICU."

Within a few hours, they decided it was not meningitis. They weren't sure what was wrong, but knew it was very serious. All kinds of doctors came to the ICU to see if they could diagnose Missie. One doctor finally recognized that Missie had a disease called thrombotic thrombocytopenic purpura (TTP). In 2004, one in three million people had the disease. The doctor explained that TTP was a disease where, for some unknown reason, your blood will start to attack itself. This doctor had seen this disease one time nine years earlier. It was a miracle to have a doctor who was not only able to diagnose the disease, but also knew what to do.

Several times a day, a machine removed all of Missie's blood, filtered it, and then put it back into her body along with some fresh "good" blood. We kept vigil in the ICU during this very critical time. We had a couple of close calls when we almost lost our girl.

Missie had a tube going down her throat and she wasn't able to speak, but we could communicate with her and she knew exactly what we were saying. One evening as we walked down the hall to ICU, Amy commented, "Missie would be horrified if she knew that I was wearing socks with my flip-flops but my feet are cold." Missie was awake, so her dad told her about the flip-flop sock situation. Missie immediately started moving her hands and shaking her head no. She wouldn't stop until Amy took those socks off her feet. Missie was our fashion consultant even from her ICU hospital bed.

Friday night came and it was time for the banquet at the old Kmart. Both BG and Amy needed to be there. BG would be sharing the vision of what that building could be and how it could function as a church. Amy was one of the children's directors and would be doing a program for the children. Some extended family members came to the hospital to stay with Missie and me. It seemed crazy to be doing a banquet in the midst of a crisis, but we really felt that it was the right thing to do.

Later that evening after my family left, I was by myself and Missie was sleeping. I stood by the window looking out, the sky was brilliant with stars. It was beautiful. In the background, I could hear the song, "How Great is our God" by Chris Tomlin playing. I stood by the window overwhelmed and yet at peace. Because God can do that in your life, can't He? In the midst of situations that are beyond our control, He gives peace. In that moment, I knew. I believed that God would heal my girl, but no matter what I would face in the days ahead, I knew that God was with me.

A wonderful group of doctors and nurses cared for Missie. By Saturday, things were beginning to look better. The nurses told us to watch the numbers displayed just over the left side of her bed. The numbers were finally looking better all day on Saturday.

Since Missie had a better day, BG decided to go home for the night. We had been at the hospital 24/7 since Wednesday. BG planned to go to church Sunday morning to let everyone know how Missie was doing. We had been at GT Church since Missie was in fifth grade. She was very involved in children's ministry. Many people had been praying for her all week long. Because Missie was improving, Amy and I urged BG to go home and actually sleep in his bed instead of on a waiting room chair.

About ten, BG left to go home and Amy and I prepared our beds. It was the first time all week that we were the only ones spending the night in the ICU waiting room. I was exhausted and went to sleep almost immediately. About midnight, I woke up and began to search for my shoes. Amy woke up too and said "Mom, what are you doing?" "I'm just going to check on Missie." She immediately said, "I'll come with you."

As soon as we turned the corner, we knew something was very wrong. Everyone—all the doctors and nurses—was in Missie's room. Missie's nurse ran over as soon as she saw us. "I was just coming to see you. Something is wrong. We are trying to work on her right now. Just wait in the waiting room and I'll come talk to you as soon as I know more."

We ran to the waiting room and called BG. He raced to get across town to the hospital.

And we waited.

The nurse came to see us occasionally, but couldn't tell us much except they were still working on Missie.

Just after 7:30 Sunday morning, a very kind doctor told us that Missie had had a brain hemorrhage. They had tried everything they could to save her, but there was no longer any brain activity. They were going to disconnect the machines that were keeping Missie alive.

We walked slowly down the hall to see her one more time.

Just before 8:00 a.m. on Sunday, October 31, 2004, our baby girl was gone.

I know at twenty-four she wasn't a baby, but you always think of your kids like that. We numbly went to the waiting room to gather our things, then headed home in complete shock and disbelief.

Our daughter. Sister. Best friend. She was gone.

ROSES AND LEAVES

Nothing prepares you for losing a child. If the child goes first, it just doesn't seem right.

As we left the hospital, BG asked, "Would it be alright if I go to the church and tell them what has happened?" First service had started. He really wanted the news of Missie's death to come from him and not someone else. I totally agreed. I didn't think I could talk to anyone right then but I definitely understood his need to tell our church family who had watched our girls grow up. The GT community had been a part of their lives for so many years.

By Sunday afternoon, we were planning Missie's funeral. Someone brought us food for lunch and our wonderful, caring staff was there to help with anything we needed. They cleaned my house so it would be ready for the family who would be arriving. Amy and I looked through pictures while BG wrote an obituary for his girl.

Two things happened that day that I will never forget. Roses and leaves. At one point during that difficult afternoon, I looked outside and saw a group of men who had come by our house to help. They hadn't even come to the door to be recognized in any way for what they were doing. They had just come to be a blessing. They were raking leaves. Large trees surrounded our house, which in late October meant lots of leaves on the ground. We had been so busy with the new building that we hadn't had time to rake, but this incredible army of men swooped in, raked the leaves, and quietly left. This one thing spoke volumes to me. Sometimes when you want to help someone in a crisis, if you see something that needs to be done, just do it. It will speak volumes of love and care.

Later that evening our doorbell rang and a small child yelled, "Trick or treat." Trick or treat? We had totally forgotten that it was Halloween. We quickly searched our cupboards for something, anything to give this little boy. As this little boy was leaving, he stooped and picked something up that was laying on our porch. BG quickly called me to come look. Someone who didn't know what to do at this time of sorrow had put roses, not rose petals but whole flowers, all down our front sidewalk. They had done the same at our back door. We were surrounded with small beautiful roses. Something about that kind act of love warmed our shattered hearts.

We decided to have the visitation and funeral on Wednesday, late afternoon and evening. More than anything we didn't want people to attend a funeral but a celebration of Missie's life. It was a beautiful service as people remembered a girl who was incredibly loving toward everyone, especially children. Missie was a fashion girl. She had an eye for beauty. She loved to help people become beautiful on the outside. She always said if people feel better about themselves on the outside, then they would feel better on the inside as well.

She was my personal fashion consultant and my beautician. Many Sunday mornings, I would have a hair emergency when I couldn't get my hair to do the right thing. I would call Missie to stop by my house on her way to church to do her thing. In less than two minutes she would have my hair emergency completely taken care of. I didn't get to see Missie every day when she moved into the apartment with Amy but we talked almost every day. Very few people had the number to the direct line in my office, but when that line rang, it was usually Missie calling just to check in.

Missie was a hugger. She loved to give hugs. That's the first thing she would do when I would see her. On Sunday mornings just after I would walk into the church building, if I hadn't had a hair emergency, Missie would be sure to come find me and give me a big, awesome hug. Now, all I could think was, "Who is going to give me a hug now?"

We had a private burial service on Thursday morning—just family and a few friends. Then it was over. Family and friends had left to go home. For most people life would go back to a regular routine, but how would we go on? How were we going to make it through the most difficult thing we had ever faced?

I was numb and lost in those first weeks after Missie died. One day I was sitting in my chair in the family room holding my Bible. I looked up my favorite verse. Jeremiah 29:11 *"For I know the plans I have for you," declares the Lord, "plans to prosper you and not to harm you, plans to give you hope and a future."*

"God, what about our verse?" Jeremiah 29:11 had been a verse I held onto through the tough times in Jacksonville, through some hard times in Grayslake, and even some difficult times in Decatur. But what now? How can the plans for my hope and a future not include my precious daughter?

Then I made a decision. Looking back, I know it was a turning point for me. I took out a journal and I began to write that verse out each morning. I would write it out and then I would write, "I still believe it."

"I still believe it."

"I still believe it."

There would be a lot of tears and struggles but I made a choice. What Satan had meant to destroy me, I was determined was not going to. I was going to choose to still trust God.

One morning after I spent time writing out my verse, God gave me a new passage of scripture:

I'll never forget the trouble, the utter lostness, the taste of ashes, the poison I've swallowed. I remember it all—oh, how well I remember—the feeling of hitting the bottom. But there's one other thing I remember, and remembering, I keep a grip on hope: God's loyal love couldn't have run out, his merciful love couldn't have dried up. They're created new every morning. How great your faithfulness! I'm sticking with God (I say it over and over). He's all I've got left. Lamentations 3:19-24 MSG

I don't ever remember reading this passage before. Maybe I had read it, but it didn't mean as much as it did that day. The beginning of this passage was describing me! It was describing exactly how I was feeling. I had just hit bottom. I was lost. The loss of my precious daughter had left me with the taste of ashes and a pain I can't describe.

As I read those passages that morning, I knew that God had given me something to hold on to. At that moment I knew I was going to make it, because God's love hadn't run out. His faithfulness was still there for me, and I was determined to keep a grip on hope! This tragedy did not take God by surprise. We were going to make it because God was going to see us through. For months following my daughter's death in 2004, I read Lamentations 3:19-24 and Jeremiah 29:11 every morning to remind myself that I was going to make it.

Maybe you are going through a hard time and you don't know where to turn and what to do next. I would encourage you to begin by reading these passages, like I did, every morning for a period of time. I believe they will give you peace and comfort for whatever you are going through.

MY BIG RED CHAIR

Before I knew it, we were at the holidays—the first holidays we would celebrate without Missie. There's no way around it. When you have lost someone special, the holidays are terribly hard.

One morning, BG came into the family room because he had an idea of what he wanted to do for me for Christmas. Truthfully, I didn't even want to celebrate and I really didn't want to talk about Christmas. But BG had an idea and wanted to talk about it.

"Brenda, why don't we get you a new chair for Christmas?"

A few years before, we had purchased a new couch and a chair for BG. At the time, my chair was fine and I opted to keep it. Now it was about twelve years old and starting to look a little worn. BG eventually convinced me that it might be good for me to have a project and pick out a new chair.

"Think about what you are going to want, and we'll go shopping on Monday."

So I really started thinking about what kind of chair I would want. Did I want a small chair with an ottoman like the one I had? I was starting to get an idea of what I wanted.

Monday morning was cold but the sun was shining as we headed out to go chair shopping. On the way to the store, BG asked, "So what kind of chair are we looking for?" To say the least, he was pretty surprised when I said, "I want a big chair. One of those new styles that will easily fit two people."

"Brenda, why do you need a big chair? You have always liked a smaller chair."

"The reason I want a large chair is because I'm getting ready."

You see, I had really been serious when I would write Jeremiah 29:11 down each day. One day, I decided to write some things down that

I believed God would do. I really did believe that God was going to give me hope and a future, so I had started writing down specific things that would be part of that future. At the top of my list was that Amy would meet an incredible guy and that BG and I would have grandchildren.

When Missie died, Amy lost her very best friend in the whole world. Amy had a lot of guys who were her friends, but she wasn't dating anyone. I knew that since Amy had been a little girl, all she wanted was to get married and have children. I also knew that grandchildren would bring joy to our home again. If I was going to buy a new chair, that chair needed to accommodate grandchildren. I wanted a chair where I could sit with my grandchildren to read books or watch movies. My chair was a step of faith. I trusted God. I was getting ready.

"Oh, did I mention I want a red chair?"

"No," BG said, "Why do you want a red chair? We really don't have anything in that room that is red."

"Well, I think red is a happy color and I've decided that I want to bring some happiness to that room where I go to spend time with God each day."

And guess what? God is so awesome. Not only did I find a red chair that would fit two people, it also was a recliner that didn't look like a recliner. And it was on sale! Yay! Sometimes God is just too good.

I had my red chair before Christmas. I've got to be honest. It didn't make those holidays any easier. We sat in our family room unwrapping gifts with tears running down our faces because of the smiling girl who was no longer present. But that chair symbolized the happiness that I believed would return to my home, and reminded me that God said we weren't done yet. He was going to do everything that He promised in Jeremiah 29:11. And I was going to be sitting in my red chair just waiting to see how He was going to do it.

I can't wait to tell you about the faithfulness of God. Missie died in the fall of 2004. Our daughter, Amy, met a wonderful guy named Derek in 2007. In 2008, she married that special guy. In March of 2010, Ella Rae (Missie's middle name) Grove was born, and in July of 2011, just sixteen months later, Bennett Grayson Grove, joined the family. I can't begin to tell you the joy these two grandchildren have brought to our family. Nothing will ever replace our sweet Missie, but God in His goodness restored the joy that our family had lost. And even more blessings are on the way. We expect Sawyer Grove to arrive in December 2015.

THE PISTOL-PACKING PREACHER

"You won't believe what happened to me today," BG said as we were fixing dinner one night. "When I went to the bank, a police officer recognized me and asked if I had a minute to talk. He asked if I would consider becoming a chaplain for the Decatur Police Department."

"What did you say?"

"Send me the paperwork that I would need to fill out and I'll check it out."

Now at the time, BG's schedule was incredibly busy. I was amazed that he was considering adding one more thing. Then he admitted, "I really told him that I would consider it because who wants to make a policeman mad? I hope he forgets to send me the paperwork. Then I won't have to make a decision on this."

But the officer did send the paperwork along with some information about becoming a police chaplain. He also invited BG to ride along with an officer just to get a feel for what chaplains do. So BG decided to give it a try to see if it was something he would even consider.

He headed out for his first ride-along on a Sunday afternoon. He had decided that Sundays from three to eleven might be the best time for him to do his shift. The first couple of hours were routine—directing traffic around an accident and helping someone with a flat tire. BG even thought they were a little boring.

Everything changed with one call. The officers responded to a home where a person with a warrant had been spotted. The officers and BG went to the front door. They knocked and identified themselves. BG, who was standing back a ways from the porch, saw a young man come out the back door and take off running. BG yelled, "We've got a runner!" The two officers and BG took off running after him. BG actually jumped a fence to try to catch him. They got him, cuffed him and put him in the squad car. That's when BG decided to sign up. He knew he was going to love being a police chaplain,

So every Sunday, BG's schedule would be to arrive at the church early and preach three services. Then he would go home, grab a quick lunch and if possible, a thirty-minute nap. Then it was off to the police station. He would arrive about 2:30 for the three-to-eleven shift. Most nights, he wouldn't be home until 11:30 or midnight. What a crazy schedule, but he loved it.

BG often said that he became a police chaplain because he loved the challenge and sometimes the adrenaline rush from chasing a criminal. But what he didn't count on was the deep respect and love he would develop for each and every officer. Everyone who worked at the department knew BG. He knew these men and women had very difficult and demanding jobs, and he was determined to bring some encouragement their way. Many times during the week, he would just stop by the police department to say hi and try to bring a smile to everyone's face.

It wasn't too long after BG had begun his Sunday ride-alongs that he realized there was a problem. A police car with a civilian (like a chaplain) could not be involved in a high-speed chase. BG immediately went in to talk to someone—anyone who could make it possible for him to sign a waiver or something so he wouldn't prevent any officer from doing his or her job. Besides, who wants to miss out on a high-speed chase? Certainly not BG Nevitt.

The department explained there was nothing they could do to alter that rule. So BG decided he was going to figure something out. That's when he realized that auxiliary officers could be in a high-speed chase. An auxiliary office is a volunteer who goes through extensive police training. After many hours of training, these men and women are then able to assist the police officers.

The next day, BG headed into the chief of police's office and asked, "What do I have to do to be an auxiliary officer?"

"I'm not sure about this," the chief said. "We have never had a chaplain who was an auxiliary officer."

"Well, let me be the first one ever."

And he was. BG went through all of the training, passed all of the tests and officially became an auxiliary officer.

Many times people asked me, "Doesn't it make you nervous that BG is out there running after people and carrying a gun?" My reply was always the same. "No, I'm so glad he is carrying a gun instead of just a flashlight."

When he was just a chaplain, BG would never stay in the car while the police were trying to deal with the bad guys. Instead, he was jumping over fences, searching houses, and looking in yards all with just a flashlight for protection. Truthfully, I was thrilled when he had all of the training. BG was a smart guy and could take care of himself in almost any situation, but now he was trained. He knew better how to help the officers he was assisting and he could also take care of himself.

BG always had a story about something that happened while he was serving with the police. Whether it was searching a house for a man who had stabbed someone, a high-speed chase (which was his favorite thing), or when his heart was broken as he held a little child whose parents were being arrested.

"Being a police officer opens your eyes to a lot of things," BG used to tell me. "You wouldn't believe some of the things that happen in our city. I can't believe how disrespectful people are to the men and women who put their lives on the line to protect them. It's amazing how the people who are cussing you out have no problem expecting you to come as soon as they have a problem."

BG spent many hours praying for the brave men and women he served alongside. There is no doubt that BG loved his "second job" with the Decatur Police Department.

AND IT ALL CAVED IN

Have you ever dropped a glass on a tile floor? It typically doesn't just break into a few pieces. Instead, it shatters into a million pieces. So many pieces that it can never be glued back together. That's what it felt like as I sat in the family room one morning in late August of 2013.

2013. The year my life fell apart and shattered into a million pieces and no matter how much super glue I used, it would never be the same again.

Maybe I should start at the beginning of the year. Although I don't usually make a New Year's resolution, I do like to begin the New Year with a feeling of a clean slate, a new beginning, a fresh start. I had high expectations for this year. I even wrote in my journal that 2013 was going to the best year ever. I felt like it was going to be a great year for me personally as well as for our church. BG and I had been at GT in Decatur for just over twenty-one years. We loved our church, and God had blessed us over the years, but I thought 2013 was going to be incredible.

The last weekend in January was our annual Refresh Women's Conference. We were expecting more than 500 women for the weekend, so there were many details to take care of before they arrived on Friday night. I was in charge of the conference and would speak on Saturday morning. Tuesday afternoon I was in a meeting when I started to feel ill. I was sure I had an infection. I'd had this before. No problem. An antibiotic would clear it up. I went to the doctor and he started me on the medicine right away, but this time I didn't get better. The antibiotic took care of the infection, but I kept getting sicker. By the time the conference began Friday night, I had given all the responsibility to other people. I was able to attend, but I sat during the worship time and only came on stage to introduce the speaker for the evening. On Saturday morning, I was the speaker for the main session. People tell me I did a very good job, but all I know is that God was carrying me through. I cannot even remember what

I said that morning. The pain was so bad that it was hard to think.

As the days went by, I continued to get worse. No one could understand why. I tried to continue to work, but in February, BG had to take me to the ER because the pain was so bad. I had no idea that would be my last day in the office for a very long time. I had begun to see specialists, but because no one knew what was causing the pain, it was difficult to know what doctors I should see.

By March, I was rarely leaving the house. The pain was overwhelming, and even strong pain pills couldn't seem to keep it in check. Then my dad called with the news that my mom was on her way to the hospital with a possible heart attack. That morning I had been in so much pain I was not able to sit up in a chair. You can imagine how helpless I felt. My sister deserves an award for stepping in to help with my mom. It was a very scary time because there were many complications with my mom's condition. One evening my sister called and told me to get to the hospital right away. My mom had a second heart attack. It was a miracle she survived that night. Throughout my mom's hospital stay, I would go to see her on my "good days" in a wheelchair. God was incredibly faithful, and my mom eventually recovered, but my journey back to health took even longer than hers.

In April, I went to Barnes Jewish Hospital in St. Louis to see if they had any answers for me. Once again because no one knew exactly what was wrong, it was difficult to choose a specialist, but God helped me to find a wonderful doctor. It was supposed to take almost four weeks to get an appointment with her, but after only one week, I got a call from her nurse telling me if I could get there that day, the doctor would see me. BG raced to drive me two and a half hours to St. Louis.

What a wonderful doctor and an answer to prayer! She didn't have answers, but she tried to do everything she could to help me. She spent more than an hour with me going over everything I had been through, and trying to come up with a plan to see if someone could help me.

Even with her help, it took months of seeing different specialists to get answers. It sometimes took four to six weeks just to get in to see the next specialist, so I would wait and pray that someone would have answers for me.

The first week in August, I was finally diagnosed with Celiac disease, which means I am very allergic to gluten. To treat this disease, I had to have a complete change of diet—for the rest of my life. When I met with the doctor who diagnosed me, she said, "Brenda, this is not causing you all of the pain you are experiencing. This diagnosis and change in diet will relieve some of your pain, but you need to realize that it is not going to take care of all of it." I looked at her and said, "If I can't eat anything good for the rest of my life, I will be well." She just laughed a bit and said, "Okay, but this still isn't going to completely cure you."

She was right and I was wrong. I guess that's why she's the specialist. The good news was the pain was not so debilitating and I could function a little better. I still couldn't walk a long distance and sometimes needed a wheel chair, but there were some things that I could begin to do like having my grandkids over to cuddle with me while we watched movies in my big red chair. For a while, I had been too sick to have them on my own, but now I felt like I could watch them for short periods while their parents prepared to move.

I felt I was finally on the road to recovery.

August 17, 2013 was a beautiful day. Amy and Derek had sold their house and were moving. The grandkids had stayed overnight with us. Ella and Bennett came down to a special breakfast that their Poppy had made them—Mickey Mouse pancakes! It was fun to start the morning off with their favorite pancakes. BG was upstairs finishing getting ready for a pastors' meeting, when it was time for me to leave with the kids. I went part way up the steps to tell him goodbye. I wanted to make sure he remembered that I was taking Bennett to my mom and dad's, and then taking Ella to her first ballet lesson. After that, I would be home to rest. I had told BG all of this earlier, but sometimes guys don't always listen to the whole conversation or don't focus in on the details—at least my guy didn't.

Just before I left, I said, "I love ya, babe! See you later!"

I dropped Bennett off, and headed to ballet with Ella. As I sat in the waiting area, my phone rang. It was our senior associate, Pastor Matt. Matt had been on staff with us for twenty years. He always called me Mama and BG, Dad.

"Mama, where's Dad?" Matt asked when I answered the phone.

"He had a pastors' meeting today. Why, do you need him?"

"No, it's okay," Matt said. "Someone just called me and said they thought he had been in an accident on his motorcycle."

"Oh Matt, he was on his motorcycle this morning."

"Wait, don't panic. Let me make a call and I will call you right back."

Don't panic was easier said than done because I was already shaking, and my mind was racing. As I turned around, there were only two other people waiting for their kids to finish ballet. One was a woman that I knew was a pastor's wife. I went to her and explained the call I had just received and asked her to pray for me. Isn't it just like God to provide someone who could pray with me at just the time I needed it? As she prayed, my phone rang again. It was Matt confirming BG had been in an accident, and telling me I needed to get to the hospital.

"Mama, do I need to have someone come get you?"

At the same time he asked me that question, a peace that only God could give came over me. I can't emphasize enough how that peace changed everything. I immediately stopped shaking and suddenly peace and confidence filled me on the inside. I knew that no matter what I had to face, God would give me the strength to do it. I told Matt, "I'm ok. I'll get Ella and meet you at the hospital."

At the hospital they immediately took me to a small waiting area where friends and family would gather. They told me BG was alive, but it was very critical. The helicopter had been called and they would be airlifting him to another hospital. As time went by, the chaplain came in again to say they were still trying to stabilize him and would be airlifting him to a larger hospital about an hour and a half away.

More friends and family were arriving to be with me when the Chief of Police came to tell me about the accident. A 19-year-old girl made a left turn. She just didn't see BG on his orange motorcycle and hit him. He had not even tried to stop because he didn't know she was going to turn into him. All I could think was *that poor girl. One of my biggest nightmares would be to injure or kill someone in an accident. I can't imagine how hard this is for her.*

A short time later, the ER doctor as well as BG's personal physician and good friend, Dr. Dan, came into the small room.

"I'm so sorry Mrs. Nevitt, we did everything we could, but we couldn't save him."

And just like that BG was gone.

I think I already knew what they were going to say. Minutes before they came in with that news, I remembered a conversation I'd had with BG a week earlier. We had gone out to dinner.

"I don't know if I have ever told you before, but when you are out of town, Amy and Derek are so good to take care of me. They always make sure that I'm alright, invite me to dinner, and just in general take care of me."

Suddenly that conversation was playing in my head. I just knew that BG knew I would be all right. He didn't have to keep fighting for his life because he knew God and my kids would take care of me. Don't get me wrong—I still believed for a miracle healing, but I felt God was saying, "He knows that you are going to be okay." When the doctors came into the room to give me the news I didn't want to hear—the news no one wants to hear—it wasn't a total shock. Just like that, the love of my life and my best friend was gone. But God had prepared my heart to hear the news.

Amy and I hugged and cried together.

"Mom, we'll be fine," Amy said. "We've been through this before and made it through. We will make it through this."

"I know we will. God will help us."

A FINAL GOODBYE

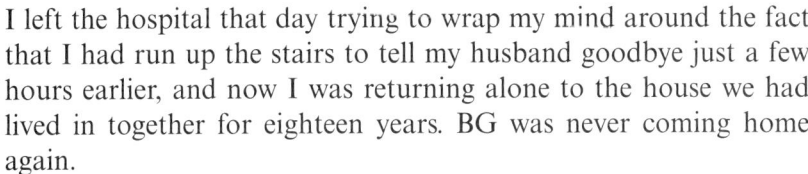

I left the hospital that day trying to wrap my mind around the fact that I had run up the stairs to tell my husband goodbye just a few hours earlier, and now I was returning alone to the house we had lived in together for eighteen years. BG was never coming home again.

Amy was right. We had been through this before and we knew what we needed to do. We called the funeral director, whom BG had worked with many times, and who had been so kind during Missie's funeral. Family and friends were notified. A lot of decisions were made quickly. When would we have the funeral? Who would be involved in the service? In the back of my mind as we went through each step of planning for the funeral, I was thinking, "It's okay. I've been down this road before. I know what has to be done." That thought was oddly comforting.

As the local news came on that night, we gathered in our family room to see what they would say about the accident. As we watched the report, they showed the license plate of the car that had hit BG. That's when Amy said, "I think I know the girl that hit Dad. I think I had her in preschool." Amy had worked as a preschool teacher all through high school and during the summer while she went to college. "I'm sure she was in the last class I taught. Her name is Elizabeth. She would have been four. I know her and her mom. Mom, she's a great girl with a really nice family." I think my heart broke a little more knowing that Amy knew this young girl. I sat there and tried to comprehend not only our loss, but also the loss and devastation that Elizabeth must be feeling.

The day had been a blur of activity. Finally, it was time to go to bed. As I walked up the stairs, it was difficult to comprehend that BG would never be sleeping with me again. His things were in the same place he had left them that morning. It didn't seem too strange for me to get ready to go to bed by myself. BG often traveled without me, and almost every Sunday night I would go to bed before he got home from his shift with the police. Many times I was asleep before he even got home. But this night was different. I decided to start some worship music and let it play through the night. This was something I had done after Missie died. It always seemed like the nights were the worst. I would miss her the most and would cry a lot so I had started to listen to worship music. It brought peace and comfort to the long nights. As I started the music, I prayed that it would help me once again and that I would be able to sleep.

I was also praying that God would give me the strength I would need for tomorrow, as well as the days ahead. I knew tomorrow would be a tough day. It was Sunday. Our family had decided that we would be at all three church services. My prayer before going to sleep was, "God, please help me to have the strength, both physical and emotional, to do what I need to do tomorrow."

I hadn't been to three services since some time in February. Over the past almost twenty-two years, I'd always attended all of the services, but when I became so sick BG would drive me to church and I would sit in a small room in the back until it was close to time for the service to start. Then someone would help me to my seat. I would sit through service and then after service was over, someone would come get me and take me home. I would sleep for a few hours just to recuperate from all the physical energy it had taken to go to church. Yes—I was that sick. Sunday was going to be an emotional and physical strain.

The news of BG's accident had been on the local news station twice on Saturday. Between the news coverage and social media, many people had heard about the accident but it happened on a weekend—a beautiful weekend—and many families had been doing things outside. They came to church having no idea that their pastor had been killed. To say the least, people were in shock! BG had been the pastor at GT for twenty-two years. He was known for greeting people with a handshake or a hug and always a big smile. He would greet everyone and encourage them to have a SPECTACULAR week.

BG was a great communicator. He had an incredible way of explaining Scripture, not only so you could understand it, but also so you could apply it to your life. I loved hearing him speak, which is a good thing since I spent years listening to his sermons three times every Sunday. I would miss him not only as my husband, but as my pastor as well.

Pastor Matt, our senior associate, did a fantastic job that morning helping the church to come to grips with what had happened. I had asked Matt specifically to talk to the church about the girl who had hit BG. She was nineteen years old and just hadn't seen BG.

"Matt, we have to tell our people that we are not going to blame this young girl for this accident. It was an accident. She did not purposely try to kill BG and we have to show her the love of Christ and in no way blame her for this accident. The people of GT have to show love and pray for this young girl. I can't imagine the pain she must be feeling now."

I was never more proud of my church family as I was that day and the days that followed as they came together and showed God's love to our community and to Elizabeth.

After the morning services, we went to the house to plan the funeral. It would be on Wednesday night—visitation at four and the service at seven—the same schedule as Missie's funeral. We did this purposely so that people would stay and be a part of the funeral. We didn't want people just to pay their respects. We were hoping that they would hear the message of Christ.

In the days before the funeral, friends helped with all kinds of practical things. Our church staff was incredible. One staff pastor who had been with us for eighteen years, had just moved to Texas. Kraig and his family immediately flew back to help. BG would have been so proud of how everyone came together to help in this time of crisis.

Wednesday arrived before I knew it and once again, I was praying for strength. I knew the hours of greeting people would be emotionally and physically taxing, and then we would still have the funeral. It's amazing how God gives you the strength you need just when you need it. That's what He did for me as hundreds of people came through the visitation line. So many people whose lives BG had touched.

One of my most emotional moments was when I looked down the line and saw uniformed police officers as far as I could see. That would have meant so very much to BG. Then the motorcycles started arriving. For years, BG had worked with the Harley Davidson dealership and conducted "Blessings of the Bikes." It started years ago with about twenty-five or thirty bikes, but had grown to thousands. The bikers organized a memorial ride across town from the Harley Davidson dealership to the church. They arranged to have streets blocked off so they could stay together as a group. The line of motorcyclists was more than four miles long. Once again, I was reminded of the number of people whose lives had been touched by BG Nevitt.

Just before seven, they told me that they had cut off the visitation line so we could get ready to go into the worship center for the funeral. I felt so bad for the people I didn't get to greet personally. Chairs and monitors had been set up in multiple locations because the worship center wouldn't hold the crowd. The local television station and the Internet made it possible for many of our friends who were not able to attend in person to still be a part of the service.

Eight to ten people were still standing in the line, when a young girl came up to me and said, "I'm so very sorry." She gave me a hug as tears rolled down her face. I didn't think much about it because hundreds of people had said the same thing to me. Amy was standing next to me. As this young girl spoke the same words to her and hugged her, Amy recognized her. It was Elizabeth. When Elizabeth realized that Amy knew who she was, the tears became sobs. I told Amy to take her to the room behind us.

I admire Elizabeth so very much. What incredible courage it must have taken to come into the church—to stand in a very long line for quite some time looking at BG's pictures and mementos as she waited. It had to be so difficult.

After I greeted the few remaining people in line, I stepped to the back and said, "Elizabeth, I want you to know I don't blame you. It was an accident. I know you didn't mean to do it. It was so courageous for you to come tonight."

It was time for the funeral to begin. I invited Elizabeth to stay for the service. I'm not sure if she stayed, but I'll never forget how incredibly brave this young girl was to come that night.

BG always said, "When I die, I want a celebration". And that's what he got. Our GT staff did an incredible job from start to finish making sure the service was everything BG would have wanted. He wanted SPECTACULAR and that's what he got.

Friends and pastors shared great stories of experiences and mission trips with BG. They talked about BG's love for life, his love for his family, and his love for the world. BG wanted to share that love with others and more than anything, he wanted people to know what God had done in his life. My daughter and son-in-law shared some incredible things that they loved about BG. His love for his family was evident in everything they shared.

But nothing prepared me for Police Chief Todd Walker's words. Let me just share a small portion of what he said that night:

"When you spend a significant time in law enforcement, you are exposed to some of the worst situations in life. You deal with so much violence and human tragedy and human despair that you become emotionally numb. You don't feel things sometimes, and you don't always trust people. As police officers, you build a protective coat of armor as a coping mechanism to survive. BG Nevitt is the only person that I have ever met in my twenty-eight years of service that was able to come into our organization full of hardened individuals and easily break down that armor and make us feel good about ourselves and about our occupation. He called us heroes every day. Treated us like heroes every day. And made us feel like heroes every day. Because of him, many of us started attending church again. Because of him, we had somebody to lean on during the times of personal stress and many of us just began to feel good again about who we were and what we did for a living. He truly was a remarkable man and had a significant presence in our lives. He was one of the first individuals that would be there if an officer was injured or in the hospital. He was one of the first to check on us if we had been involved in a significant or dangerous situation. He was one of the first to be there when we were celebrating the birth of a new child and sometimes he was called to perform marriages and unfortunately

funerals for some of the officers that had passed away whether they were active duty or retired. He was viewed by many as our "Superman" because he was everywhere we needed him to be at every time.

"I often had the opportunity to just sit and have a conversation with him. I felt so comfortable around him I didn't fear joking with him. And I often made fun of the shoes he wore – and the shirts – and sometimes even the jeans. I didn't fear my language when speaking with him. I could ask him anything and he was genuinely concerned about my family and me. There was one question that I asked him that I will never forget and that was about his energy level. As many of you know, BG was full of energy and it was no different at the police department. I know it is hard to believe but at the police department, we aren't always just smiling or having fun but anytime BG graced us with his presence, he was always smiling, always full of energy and always spectacular. I asked him how he found it within himself to be so vibrant and full of energy. I joked with him one time just shortly after I became chief of police three years ago. I said, 'Look I don't need a scandal as the chief of police. You need to cut back on Mountain Dew or some kind of energy drink.' After he chuckled, he leaned into me with a large smile and said, 'I have energy because I love my life. I love living – you ought to try and get you some because it's absolutely wonderful.'

"That answer has always stuck with me and even though I haven't always lived up to his expectations, I only hope one day that I can become a fraction of the man he was to us and so many in the community. BG often expressed how blessed he was to be a part of the Decatur Police Department but what he did not realize that the blessing was truly ours. He was one of us. He was our tactical Chaplain, our Pistol Packing Preacher, our biggest supporter and our friend. His tour of duty is over with us. He will forever be missed but we will continue on with our mission because that is what he would want us to do."

His words touched my heart in a way that is hard to describe. I guess you never know how deeply you've impacted others. I was blessed by the love of the countless people who reached out to our family after BG's death.

THIS WAS NOT THE PLAN

"What's the plan?" If you are around me very long at all, you will hear me ask this question. I do not have to be the person who makes the plan, but I like to know the plan. What are we doing today? Where are we going to eat? What is the plan? I just like to know.

The question, "What's the plan?" is now constantly on my mind, because I did not think the plan was that at fifty-five I would be a widow. I also hadn't planned on losing my youngest daughter or being very sick and in need of lots of pain medication just to make it through the day. On a good day, I could walk short distances, but if I was able to go to Wal-Mart, I had to use one of those motorized scooters. If you have ever driven one of those, you know they aren't easy to maneuver, especially at the end of the aisles when you can't see around the corner.

I had a plan. My plan was that BG and I would grow old together and still act like we were young. Our girls would grow up and marry wonderful men who loved Jesus and their families. We would have awesome, incredible grandchildren and enjoy every minute that we got to spend with them. BG loved to travel so he would travel and speak. I was going to spend my time with the grand kids and travel with BG when I wanted to. It was a great plan, wasn't it?

Now I had no plan and it felt like all I did was cry. Amy, Derek, and my grandkids, Ella and Bennett moved into my house. Having them there has made a huge difference. Two grandchildren, ages two and three, made the days go by quicker, but I was still physically exhausted and a long way from being well. Not feeling well made the sadness of losing BG even worse. Each day was a great challenge for me.

In place of a plan, I had questions.

Will I have enough money to live on?

Where will I live?

Will I be well enough that I will be able to go back to work?

What will happen with my job?

So many questions and no answers and no one to tell me what the plan was. BG had always been the one with the plan and now I was all alone.

So I decided I was going to do what I had done when Missie had died. I remembered that I just kept focusing on a couple of scripture passages. This time, I would start with Ephesians 3:20. If you knew BG very long at all, you would know this was his favorite verse because it has such a powerful and encouraging message to it. We even had bracelets made with E3:20 on them for his funeral. He liked the words in any version, but it was The Message version he most often quoted, so it was the first verse I would turn to everyday.

God can do anything, you know—far more than you could ever imagine or guess or request in your wildest dreams!

Then I would read Lamentations 3:19-30. I like The Message version for this passage, too, because it reminds me, "God is faithful."

I'll never forget the trouble, the utter lostness, the taste of ashes, the poison I've swallowed. I remember it all—oh, how well I remember—the feeling of hitting the bottom. But there's one other thing I remember, and remembering, I keep a grip on hope: God's loyal love couldn't have run out, his merciful love couldn't have dried up. They're created new every morning. How great your faithfulness! I'm sticking with God (I say it over and over). He's all I've got left.

Finally, I would read my favorite verse, Jeremiah 29:11.

"For I know the plans I have for you", declares the Lord, "plans to prosper you and not to harm you, plans to give you hope and a future."

Each day, I would read my verses and say just what I said after Missie died. "I still believe it. I don't understand why this happened. I'm not sure how I'm going to make it through but I still believe it."

One morning as I sat in my big red chair, I remembered something a good friend of mine had said. Her family was going through a very difficult time. It seemed like every day things were getting worse. The more they tried to do what they thought was right and honorable, the worse things got. It was so bad that she didn't even want to get out of bed because she was afraid of what the new day would hold. So she decided that each day before she got out of bed, she would say, "God, I trust you. God, I trust you. I don't understand all we are going through but I trust you." She told me that sometimes she would have to almost shout those words out before she could make herself get out of bed, but declaring her trust in God out loud gave her the assurance that she needed to remember that He had never let her down before, and He wouldn't leave her when she needed Him the most. I knew I needed to say that phrase out loud myself. I began saying, "God, I trust you," not only in the morning, but many times during the day.

One morning as I said those words, I remembered my favorite story in the Bible. It's the story of Joseph. I love that story so much that I decided to pull out my Bible and read it again. This time I was really going to think about how many times it would have been easy for Joseph to give up, throw in the towel, and say, "God, I'm done. Life's too hard. Things didn't go according to my plans." He had to choose to say over and over again, "God, I trust you." Well, it doesn't say in the Bible that he actually said those words, but as I read the story, I'm convinced that there were a lot of days in his life that he had to say those words.

You can read the story beginning in Genesis 37 but let me give you the Brenda Nevitt version:

From the beginning, Joseph's family could have been labeled dysfunctional with a capital D. His daddy was married to two women who were sisters. You can see where that could be trouble. To make things even worse, Daddy only truly loved one of his wives, and that was Rachel. Joseph was Rachel's son and Daddy adored him.

If you heard the story in Sunday school about the coat of many colors that probably had been purchased at Nordstrom's, Joseph was the boy who got that coat. He got the great new coat while his brothers from another mother had to wear clothes from the thrift store or hand-me-downs. The other brothers had to work hard for

Daddy but Joseph didn't have to do much of anything because he was Daddy's favorite. Joseph's job was to tattle on the other brothers if they weren't doing what they were supposed to do. Sounds like the perfect family situation.

To make things even worse, Joseph had a couple dreams where everyone, including his brothers, bowed down to him. Joseph decided to share this news with his whole family. That news just made the brothers hate this golden boy all the more.

One day, when Joseph was seventeen, Daddy told him to go out to the fields to check up on his brothers. The brothers saw him coming a long way off and decided they had had it with this daddy's boy. They decided to kill him and take that fancy coat covered with blood back to daddy and tell him a wild animal killed his little golden boy. Pretty extreme!

But they didn't kill Joseph. Instead, they sold him into slavery. Joseph's day had started out just like a regular day and suddenly his brothers sold him into slavery. He was seventeen. He'd never done anything for himself and now he was a slave in a country where he didn't even know the language. He was totally alone—no family, no friends, nobody except God. And Joseph grew up to be a bitter man who hated everyone because of what his brothers did to him—right?

He didn't! He could have. People would have understood if he had carried a chip on his shoulder and only through years of counseling been able to let it go. Instead, at some point after the shock of his life being turned upside down, I believe Joseph said, "God, I trust you. I don't understand this. I thought you gave me a dream and now I'm a slave, but I trust you." And then the Scripture says, "The Lord gave him success in everything he did." He found favor in a high-ranking official's house. He was put in charge of all the other slaves and everything in the entire household. I'm sure he was confident then that God was going to turn all things for good in his life.

Out of nowhere, the high-ranking official's wife accused Joseph of rape. She had been after him for a while because she thought he was a fine looking young guy, but Joseph kept doing the right thing. She got so mad that she framed him for rape and he ended up in jail.

For doing the right thing!

It doesn't seem right, does it? At this point, I think Joseph has to say, "God, I trust you. I did the right thing so surely you won't allow them to keep me in jail for long." I'm sure that got harder to say and to believe as days and weeks and years went by. In the midst of it all, Joseph found favor with the prison warden and was put in charge at the jail. At some point, Joseph helped a couple of guys in the jail by interpreting some dreams. Both men had worked for the Pharaoh, the king of Egypt. They had offended Pharaoh and ended up in jail. When Joseph interpreted the dreams, he said to one, "I'm sorry but your dream shows you will die." To the other one, he said, "You will be given your job back. When you get back to the palace, will you let them know I'm in prison for something I didn't do?" I'm sure Joseph thought that this would be how God would get him out of prison. It wouldn't be long now. But it was more than two years before anything would change for Joseph.

"God, I trust you!" On day number 730, I'm sure he woke up saying it one more time. "God, I don't see how you are going to do it. I don't know how you are going to turn things around in my life, but I trust you. I know you gave me those dreams and someday they will become true in my life.

And those dreams did come true! Joseph woke up one morning in the jail. It was just like any other morning. There was no warning anything had changed, but suddenly someone came running to the jail and told the warden to get Joseph cleaned up because Pharaoh wanted to see him. Pharaoh had a dream and wanted to have Joseph interpret that dream. Just like that, Joseph was standing in front of Pharaoh. He interpreted the dream for Pharaoh. Joseph told him, "There will be seven years of abundance throughout the land of Egypt, but seven years of famine will follow. The abundance in the land will not be remembered because the famine that follows will be so severe."

Then it happened. Pharaoh said something that astounded Joseph. Here's what it says in Genesis 41:39:

"Since God has made all this known to you, there is no one so discerning and wise as you. You shall be in charge of my palace, and all my people are to submit to your orders."

Wow. I'm sure Joseph's head was spinning. God had changed everything in a blink of an eye. And I think it was because Joseph all along was saying, "God, I trust you".

That story always inspires me and it did that day. As I thought of my friend's story and Joseph's story, I began to think, "God, I trust you."

I don't understand this. I don't know how I'll get through this but I trust you and I will continue to trust you on the days when I feel alone and on the days I feel brokenhearted, I will choose to remind myself that I trust you.

ONE STEP AT A TIME

It has not been easy but God has been faithful as I take one step at a time. Grief can be overwhelming and consuming. It's a process that you have to go through. I know it because I have been through this before. But it is hard.

BG was my world. We were not only married but we worked together. We spent most of our time together. We ate lunch and dinner together almost everyday. We decided years ago to skip trying to have breakfast together. BG wasn't a morning person and I am, so most days we would eat breakfast on our own. We loved to spend time together. We dreamed about the future together. Now my world had crashed and shattered all around me.

"Mrs. Nevitt, could you fill out this paperwork?" Just over a week after BG passed away, I was at a business that needed me to update my information. I just sat there with the pen in my hand and couldn't move to fill out the form. For more than thirty-six years, I had checked "Mrs." on forms. Now I sat with the pen in my hand trying to make myself move the pen over to mark "Widow." I wonder if I'll ever get used to checking that box.

In the midst of the grief, I decided I would try to look for things I could be thankful for and write them in my journal. My friend, Kelli, had sent me a note about a crisis her family had gone through. In the midst of that crisis, she had begun to look at the blessings that were around her and to write them down. One terrible event had changed everything. The terrible situation was still there, but she had put things in perspective when she looked at the blessings God had provided in the midst of it all.

It changed things for me, too. When I was overwhelmed and didn't think I could go on, I tried to stay focused on how God was providing for me and how he was bringing joy in the midst of sorrow.

I was still struggling with my health. I still had very bad pain in my lower abdomen that no one could explain. Changing my diet to gluten free had helped, so I was at least able to get out of bed and do a few things, but I still had so much pain. The doctors believed that something catastrophic had happened in my body in January 2013, and that had set off the Celiac disease as well as other things that were causing the pain and fatigue. I continued to go to Barnes Jewish Hospital to see if specialists would have any answers, but they had none.

By the end of September, I was back at the church working part-time. It was a real struggle, but I was doing it. It took me a long time to walk to my office—physically and emotionally. My office was right next to BG's so each day was very emotional, and walking down the long halls of our large church was a physical challenge. I pushed myself to go to work. When I got home, I immediately went to bed.

In the months following BG's death, my life completely changed. My daughter, son-in-law, grandkids and I decided to move to a house where we could all live together. We wanted a place where all of us could have our own space but still be together, and we found it. The house was in a great neighborhood near awesome schools, and it had the space we needed. It was a foreclosure, which can sometimes be a difficult sales process to navigate, but God was faithful and the sale went through quickly. We got the house for a great price. It had been vacant for more than three years. There was no reason that house shouldn't have sold. I know God was keeping it just for us.

January 2014 was here before I knew it and it was time for our annual Refresh Women's Conference. God had given me the strength to plan the event with the help of my daughter, Amy. It was Saturday morning and the conference had been going incredibly well. I was the speaker for the final session. It would be my first speaking engagement in a year. I would still need to sit in a chair. My message that morning would be "What To Do When It All Caves In." For the first time, I was going to talk about my health, losing BG, and losing Missie. I was going to share those incredibly hard things that had happened in my life. But more importantly, I was going to share the hope that God was giving me in the midst of the struggle.

As I got into my car to drive home after the conference, I was happy that God had touched so many lives, and relieved that I had made it through the weekend. As I reached to start my car, I had a strong impression from God. In my mind, I heard the words, "You will take that message all over the world to give hope and encouragement to others." I said aloud, "God, I will do what you have asked me to do, but you'll have to make me well."

In April of 2014 an answer to my health problems came in a very unexpected way. I received a message from a woman who goes to my church. Sandy said she had read an article in *Prevention* magazine about something that causes a lot of pain in the lower abdomen. Her note said, "I don't even know exactly what symptoms you are experiencing, but I just felt like I was supposed to pass this information on to you."

I pulled up the article and as I started reading, I realized that I had almost every one of the symptoms it described. Oh my goodness! Could this be my answer? I immediately began researching to see what kind of doctors diagnosed this type of condition. I needed to find a specialist in a very specified field. And I found one.

The next day, I called to make an appointment. Frankly, I was prepared for a long wait to get into see this new doctor. It had been taking four to six weeks between each specialist in St. Louis and I had been told this doctor was extremely busy so it might take even longer to get in. They said, "Could you be here on Thursday, April 13th?" I immediately said, "Yes" as I quickly wrote down the information. Then I stopped.

"Do you mean tomorrow?"

"Yes, I just had a cancellation before you called."

I couldn't believe it. The very next day I was on my way to see if this doctor would have answers for me. "God, please give this doctor wisdom to help me today."

I met with the resident before I actually saw the doctor. I told her my story of almost a year and a half of pain, including my self-diagnosis from the article in *Prevention* magazine. She looked at me and said, "If you have it, he will know. That is what he specializes in."

After a thorough exam and hearing all I had been through, the doctor looked at me and said, "You have Pelvic Floor Dysfunction." I almost jumped off the table and hugged him. I had a name! Someone knew what was wrong with me! Not only did he know what was wrong, but he also knew how to help me. He was confident that physical therapy along with medication would make a huge difference in my life.

I was so excited. I would have to come to St. Louis for my physical therapy, which was a two-and-a-half-hour drive from my house, and I didn't care. I didn't care if they said I needed to make that trip every day. I would find a way. God had directed me to a doctor who knew how to help me and I was so very grateful.

And I began to slowly get better. I was able to work out a physical therapy schedule in St. Louis and do a lot of it on my own at home. God was using the doctors and physical therapists to pour healing into my body. It wasn't an overnight healing, but each day I was doing better. I was getting stronger. Thank you, God, for your healing power!

LIVE LIKE YOU WERE DYING

I went sky diving,

I went rocky mountain climbing,

I went 2.7 seconds on a bull named Fu Manchu.

And I loved deeper,

And I spoke sweeter,

And I gave forgiveness I've been denyin',

And he said someday I hope you get the chance,

To live like you were dyin'.

"Live Like You Were Dying," written by Tim Nichols and Craig Wiseman and sung by Tim McGraw, was playing on the radio as BG and I exited the Phoenix airport in our rental car several years ago. BG said, "I have to get that song. I want to hear it again."

I can't tell you how many times we listened to that song while we were in that rental car. Over and over we heard that message in those lyrics. Almost every time we listened to it, BG would tear up. Okay, sometimes I would, too. I guess it just hit both of us that you never know how long you have on this earth, so you'd better make the most of it.

Living life like you are dying is different from living life without regrets. We all have some regrets—things we can't go back and fix. One thing I admired about BG was that at some point, he decided he was going to live life to the fullest. On that Saturday morning in August, as he lay in the emergency room, I don't think he was full of "I wish..." I think he was content with the life he had lived. He had lived a life loving God. He loved his family, the church he served, and the Decatur Police Department. He had traveled the world, and had done things he thought he could never do. God had given him numerous opportunities, and even when he was uncertain or afraid, he had stepped up and done what needed to be done.

If he were here right now, BG would encourage you to decide to live like you were dying. Take time to think about what you want your life to look like at the end, and start living it. Be sure that God is your number one priority. If you don't have time for the people and the things that are the most important, BG would tell you it's time to change your priorities. Don't let fear hold you back from what you want to do in this life. Sometimes you just have to do it afraid.

And if you have never taken the step to ask Jesus to come into your life, there is no better day than today. I can't imagine going through life without having the strength and peace that only God can give. I would encourage you right now to take that step and pray the prayer that BG said at the end of every church service. As you pray, just mean it with all your heart.

Father God, I come to you because I need you. I admit that I have sinned, and I ask you to forgive me of every sin. Lord Jesus, come into my life, be my Lord, be my Savior, be my King. I give you my all today, and I choose to live for you every day for the rest of my life. Thank you Lord, for the new life and the new beginning that I have right now through Jesus Christ, my Lord and Savior. Amen.

If this is the first time you have prayed that prayer, you have made the best decision you will ever make in your life. I encourage you to find a good church that will help you understand what it means to have a relationship with God.

I always thought BG's line, "This is going to make a great story," was about the adventures: the near misses on a plane or the terror in a foreign country. But I realize that the story I tell now, about the faithfulness of God no matter what comes my way, is also a great story.

I absolutely love happy endings. I wish I could write "and she lived happily ever after." No more challenges. No more tears. Life has been difficult so far but now there will be no more heartache. No more disappointments. But that's not how life will be for any of us.

John 16:33 says, *"In this world you will have trouble."* But the verse doesn't stop there. The rest of the verse says, *"But take heart! I have overcome the world."*

As long as we live in this world, we are going to have trouble. I love what author Holly Gerth said:

"We don't have a choice about the rain that comes into the pathway of our dreams, but we can choose what we do with it and what we let it do to us."

There will be more rain. But as difficulties, challenges, and sometimes great heartaches come our way, each of us gets to decided how we will handle it. We get to choose our response. We can let the rain completely take us out or we can choose to dance in the rain, not because of the circumstances but in the midst of the circumstances.

I hope you decide to dance in the rain.